how to
CONDUCT
SPIRITUAL
WARFARE

as I see it !

by Mary Garrison

Contents

1
As I See It

Have you wondered lately why so many of God's servants are suddenly becoming writers? And have you also noticed how many of those servants are writing books on spiritual warfare, demons, and what to do about it? Yes, God has constrained many of us who have been trained by the Holy Ghost in schools of experience - to inform as many of the household of God as possible.

Don't be deceived by those who will not hear what the Spirit is saying to the Church in this day. If there were only a scattered few proclaiming these truths to the Church, we could assume it not to be important. But, when thousands are being called to arms - and sounding the trumpet in Zion, then **that** is what the **SPIRIT** is saying to the Church.

Yes.:.there is a great stirring about in the household of God these days. You need only to go into the Christian bookstores and look upon the shelves to confirm what I am saying, or tune in on any religious radio channel. You will hear ministers of God preaching and trying to get the message over. There is a great purpose to all of this information. The devil, his false prophets, the deceived and the deceiver, has declared war upon the Saints of God. And, these evil ones are and will be prevailing against the saints.

God, as I see it, has started a preparation. He is raising up a mighty overcoming army who will go forth in overcoming power - taking blood bought victories out of Satan's hands. They will take the Kingdom by force. That is the only way they will take it. Satan and his demons will not give up the souls of men without a battle.

Now, as I see it, no one writer or preacher necessarily has all of the truth. But, most of them have an important contribution to our information. God has told many of these servants to write.

We must learn how to try a spirit so that we can "eat the meat and spit out the bones", as a brother put it. When God told me to write **HOW TO TRY A SPIRIT**, He showed me that while I was reaching hundreds by ministering and speaking, I could reach thousands by writing. Also, He will protect much of these continuing Acts of the disciples for the aid of those that are here when that terrible, tribulous time, is upon the face of the earth.

You, brethren, who want to be conscientious objectors to this mighty spirtual battle, hear this: You can be if you choose, but take a look at page 31 in **HOW TO TRY A SPIRIT**, at the rewards promised by Jesus to those who overcome! Want to miss that? Not me!

A prophecy was spoken during the Conference on Pentecost in 1975. It is a word we need to hear in this hour. Also, it is a word we need to obey. It is a Word of God that should be shared with all of God's family. It is this conviction that leads me to make a closer analysis and share my comments with you.

The Prophecy

"I speak to you of the dawn of a "new age" for My Church. I speak to you of a day that has not been seen before...**Prepare yourselves** for the action that I begin now, because things that you see around you will change; the combat that you must enter now is different; it is new. You need wisdom from Me that you do not yet have. You need the power of My Holy Spirit in a way that you have not possessed it; you need an understanding of My will and of the **ways that I work** that you do not yet have. Open your eyes, open your hearts to prepare yourselves for Me and for the day that I

2

have now begun."

My analysis and comments upon this prophetic word:

1. "Prepare yourself." He did not say wait on Him and He would prepare you. No...He said: You train **yourself** for war! - for action. When: Now. Why? Things are changing. How? The fighting **you must do** is different. **In what way?** It is to be a spirit to spirit battle. We do not wrestle flesh and blood, but principalities of of the air; so therefore, God is revealing the proper warfare tactics through the enlightenment of certain servants. The Bible states, He will not do anything without first telling his servants. So it is not enough to hearken to the prophets, we must also react. (Amos 3:7)
2. "You need wisdom from Me that you do not yet have." He said you need more knowledge about this new combat that you will now enter into. You need to know who you are to battle, their names, their methods, what they are fighting over. Down through the ages, God has used man inspired by the Holy Ghost to speak to His People.
3. "You need the power of My Holy Spirit in a way that you have not possessed it; you need an understanding of My will and of the ways that I work that you do not yet have."
4. Important instructions: God, in speaking, gives information on things to come and strict instructions on what to do. He says do this: "Open your eyes."

Many leaders are allowing Satan to keep them blinded to this great spiritual warfare that is in the world. Many of the people under them are being affected by this new and different combat that this prophecy warns us about. But the blind cannot lead the blind. God has not allowed this combat to come upon us without proper preparation of His servants. Many of God's seasoned servants have been given certain truths. The scriptures have been opened up to them in such a way that they have the necessary wisdom needed to overcome the enemy. God has been preparing them for many years. God has commanded that they write in a book the information, instructions, and knowledge needed for this time. "well...then", you say," just **WHAT** is the problem?"

5. "Open your eyes, open your hearts, to prepare yourselves for Me and for the day that I have now begun." This is the problem Saints: God's servants obeyed after years of careful preparation, training by the Holy Ghost, fasting and prayer. They wrote the books. The books were on the market. But the people's eyes and hearts were closed, and many rejected the preparation.

My books, **HOW TO TRY A SPIRIT**, and **HOW TO CONDUCT SPIRITUAL WARFARE**, are only a small part of this preparation plan. But it is an important part in that it takes the veil off and reveals the true names and fruits of the strongmen and how to resist them. Throwing the spotlight upon the dark forces, **WE** are expected to overcome until the end.

The Bible says the gates of hell cannot prevail against the Church. That is to say the gates of hell are not strong enough to stand up under a direct attack, or onslaught, of the Church that may be on the offensive to capture some of hell's victims. Some people seem to be of the opinion that the gates of hell are supposed to start pushing and assaulting the gates of the Church and that if we don't antagonize them, we will be safe within the walls. I say this is a reversal of what God intends for us. Why did He give us the whole Armour of God and the Sword; power over all their power; great weapons of warfare, mighty through God to the pulling down of all their strongholds? To keep peace with Satan and his demons? I should say not! To fight! To storm the gates of hell and to put the devil to flight. So...get off your pews...Church, and start.

Invading   Persuading   and   Prevailing!

4

2
Quest for Spiritual Realities

It is instinctive in man to desire to know the unknown. He knows that there is much more in existence than what meets the natural eye. He has seen psychic operations, healings, and many other amazing supernatural phenomena displayed. One can hardly pick up a newspaper, turn on a television, or visit a book store, and not be aware of this fact.

For years I have observed an intense interest arising in the majority of people to know more about the spirit world. They look at a dead body and realize the person is no longer there. Where did the spirit go?

I believe that all intelligent human beings are intensely interested in "unseen" things. This point is proved by the sales slips of occult literature. I read in **Writer's Magazine** that many writers are beginning to zero in on this market. One article I recently read by an author of many such books stated she was neither a psychic or medium, but wrote for the money--basing her research on older books.

People are turning to those who believe a lie because mature Christians are not publishing the truths that are far more exciting. This multitude of people are searching for realities. Yes...for the truth which many mature Christians hold in silence! My heart breaks at the sight of what I see in this situation. That Gospel truth we are supposed to be shouting from the housetops is what these are after!

They are indeed upon a quest to find spiritual realities. Most of the time the church or ministers are **THEIR FIRST EFFORTS.** You may not realize it, but interview those who have turned to the occult for answers, and you will see that this is a fact. The occult leaders actually give them a part truth. (which is more than they received from us.) Where did the occult get their part truths? Out of the Bible, of course.

God gave the church gifts to equip and perfect the saints unto every good work. The church is supposed to meet all of the spiritual needs of the seekers. Yet many a seeker comes to us for help, and we refer them to a psychiatrist, physician, etc. Finding no spirtual help and answers there, either, the seeker may seek unto one having a **familiar spirit**--a medium or witch, and find more information there than he found in the Church! Brethren, this ought not to be! God has given us wisdom, revelation knowledge, the gifts, the Truth. All the keys to the Kingdom are ours.

While the church of God remains mute on the existence of demons, scores of people turn to the occult. The witch covens in town grow fatter each week. I do not believe that God is pleased with such a cop-out of an ignorant church! Only knowing the Truth will set people free! All of this bar-breaking Truth that we shall ever need is contained in that precious Book Christians carry around.

This truth must be held forth to the people in righteous-ness, while living a righteous life applying this truth. Fear of public opinion causes most ministers to avoid educating themselves on deliverance for the oppressed. They do not want to lose esteem with their peers. Shouldn't we be more concerned with pleasing the One who chose us to soldier for Him? Take a look at His example for us concerning the deliverance miracle ministry. Then follow Him in that example regardless of the consequences...You are sure to please Him!

If you care to search out the facts under the revelations of the Holy Ghost, you will have more exciting truths, miracles, facts about spiritual beings, death, after death, soul travel, spiritual warfare, supernatural powers, language, every power gift, etc. that would satisfy to the fullest every quest that a seeker could possible have in their inner-most being!

I have found that there is no end to God's adventure in the spiritual realm. As I seek I find. As I knock He answers. When I push on a door, it opens. I can go as fast and far as I am ready in God's Truths. If God knows, I can know. If I do not know, I ask God. He does not upbraid me--He tells me. After all, I'm being conformed into the likeness of His Son.

If someone comes to me and ask if I can help them, if I can answer a question, I say, "Of course, I can. You have surely come to the right place. I can do **all** things through Christ who strengthens me. The Kingdom of God is **at hand**. (within me.) If Jesus says it's there, it's there. What do you want of God?" Bold! That's what we need--Holy Boldness.

If they need an answer and go to the medium, what do you think she will say? "I'm sorry, my dear, we should not delve into those things, we might get into error as some of those way-out Christians are!" I should say not! She will answer them with satanic knowledge!

Aren't we supposed to have power and knowledge **over** all theirs?

Then what is the problem? Where have we failed?

The moment a mature Christian begins to publish c preach these truths, all hell breaks loose. The Devil himself stirs up many ministers to come against him. Put out little hints, little comments, little insinuations, little smears, a wag of the head, a lofty look. Satan's strategy is just this:

> 1. Kill his influence,
> 2. Discredit him,
> 3. Cut him off at the onset.

Satan doesn't dare use witches against him openly, then the Christians would recognize the enemy and fight together. No, he uses the Brethren who do not know a demon from an angel, and are too haughty to learn, unteachable, dogmatic, never coming to the Truth. Now let me tell you how it is. For laying your tongue upon that

7

annointed ministry you come under a curse. And now we come to why many Christians are weak, sick, and powerless. If we manage to get out from under these curses, then we are going to come into the power of God!

The saints, who believe, shall overcome Satan with the **word** of their testimony, the Blood of Jesus, and the fact that they love not their lives unto the death! Are we so concerned with our lives, reputations, and careers that we are losing the battle? Without the confrontation there is no victory.

Witches act like the Devil! Let us act like God!

3
The Gifts of Discerning of Spirits

"Lord, I pray that you would open his eyes that he may see." Elisha

The gift of **Discerning of Spirits** is hard to describe, but I think there is a great need for us to try. When I received the gift of **Discerning of Spirits**, it was as if I had been spiritually blind, but suddenly received my sight. It enabled me to serve God in a far greater capacity. Now when I minister, I can see the problem and react properly.

This gift opened to me the whole supernatural realm of the spirit world. I could see with my "spirit eyes" exactly what was happening in the spirit realm. I could see the evil spirits, their motives, their crafty tricks and devices. I could see the leadings of the Holy Spirit; how He wanted to use me, and what He wished to accomplish in a given situation, to bring about the Holy Spirit's purpose in the meeting. Thus, the spiritual victories exceed ordinary accomplishments for the Kingdom of God.

At these times, I can see everything going on in the room. I can see the needs people have that God desires to meet. I can see how the evil spirits use not only sinners, but saints too, to stop these needs from being met. I have seen seasoned ministers lend themselves to satan by changing the subject just when the seeker is ready to receive, or perhaps unknowingly block the direction the Spirit wants to take. We must realize that both powers use man to accomplish their wills and we are a servant to whom we yield our members! We are a deciding factor as to how the battle goes.

The **Discerning of Spirits** also shows which gifts of the

Holy Spirit are manifesting in a service. The person with the gift knows how God is working; he also knows how evil spirits are working. If the saints would recognize the gift of **Discerning of Spirits** in the church and allow it to operate, the church would accomplish more. It would be safer. There would not be as many perverse, false spirits running our churches.

Discerning of Spirits is able to judge the gifts, to know if they are genuine. This judgment certainly should not be left to one who does not understand spiritual things and fights God's power and gifts...yet how many novices do we see over the people? When God builds the Church, the gates of hell will not prevail against it. Do you know why? Those gifts He gave us for perfecting the saints are Gods' own powers! Jesus ascended on high, and gave gifts to men...far superior to anything satan can muster up, or the abilities of mere man.

The gift of **Discerning of Spirits** cannot be compared to any natural ability of man to discern, sense, or imagine, nor make educated guesses...about a person. Discerning **people** is not the purpose of this gift at all, but it is to discern one spirit from another by name.

Who are these spirits? Is it God? The Holy Spirit? An angel? A demon? The devil himself? A good ministering spirit? A familiar spirit? If evil spirits are present, what are they doing? If they are there, you better believe they are up to something. They have a plan and will execute that plan successfully if no one resists them. Saints, this is important to know! If evil forces use their power to do evil; that evil stands until such a time as a stronger power overpowers them. Can you see why we should not be idle during this war? We need to be undoing heavy burdens, loosing bands of wickedness, breaking curses spoken by evil human spirits, and letting the oppressed go free!!

When Elisha was describing the way the battle was lining up to his servant, he could count more spirits to help them than soldiers to come against them. He **SAW** the armies of God! When the gift of **Discerning of Spirits** is in operation, we too can see the battle rage over the souls of men. It is as if the way the battle goes depends upon the way we fight. The believer can command both sides. The Bible says, ''The spirits are subject to **US!**'' What an awesome responsibility! It's true though, ''We have power over their power.'' But we must **use** that power. We must take the Kingdom by force. **The Keys to the Kingdom are Binding and Loosing!** Mt. 16:19; 18:18

Discerning of Spirits is a powerful gift that incorporates the gifts and attributes of God to give the worker a ''God's eye view'' of all situations. When that gift is in operation in my ministry, I no longer am operating on man level, man knowledge, nor man power; but I find that I have entered into God power, God knowledge, and God **sight**. Nothing is withheld from me. If I am counseling someone, I see their need from beginning to end. Usually it has no relation to what they are telling me at the time. It is as if their lives become transparent to me and I ''discern'' them, but only what God wants me to see and act on. Never are private and personal matters that are none of my business revealed, except when God wishes to expose them. So...if I see it, God has revealed it for **their** good.

We do not operate that gift. The Holy Ghost in us is in charge of the gift. He decides what, when, and where. **We** try spirits by fruit and get good results, but, this Divine gift carries us far beyond all of that! It is given to perfect the saints, get them ready for Him, therefore, the veil is lifted **only** by God, the Holy Ghost, who leads and guides us into all truth!!!

4
How to Try a Spirit

It is important that everyone should know how to try a spirit by it's fruit. I have found that the ability to correctly try a spirit is of the utmost importance to me in the ministry. I am convinced that this knowledge is a must for Christians. I also am thoroughly impressed with the need for more insight on the part of Christians in such matters, that I believe I have a Holy unction from God to convey and reveal this knowledge to as many as possible.

The Holy Spirit has confirmed this commission by giving me Divine assistance in this mission beyond any measure that I have imagined.

I have not always had this knowledge of how to try a spirit. In fact, I didn't receive it until after I had received the Gift of God -- the Discerning of Spirits.

Before I learned ''how to'', I was deceived many times. I suffered much because of the fact that I did not know how to try a spirit. I had never heard anyone teach on this subject. When I tried to find out, they would give me some Scriptures, but that didn't really tell me how to know them either. Although some did tell me to try a spirit by it's **fruit**, I still did not know what **fruit** belonged to which spirit. Therefore, I was deceived many times without realizing it. I also fell into a few satanic entrapments because of this lack of knowledge. The Holy Ghost always brought me out of these snares, teaching me the truth, thank God! Most of these experiences that I suffered could easily have been avoided had I known these facts about spirits.

So...''Come and buy gold from me,'' tried in the furnace of affliction.

The Bible tells us that in these last days, the very elect of God will be deceived if it were possible for satan to do so. And it is not only possible, but easy, if we are going to disobey the Word, and believe every spirit that comes to us as being from God, not bothering to try them, as instructed to do.

Let us review in Matthew 7:15 what Jesus said:

"Beware of false prophets which come to you in sheeps clothing but inwardly they are ravening wolves. You shall know them by their fruits. Do men gather grapes of thorns, or figs of thistles? Even so every good tree bringeth forth good fruit. But a corrupt tree bringeth forth evil fruit. A good tree cannot bring forth evil fruit, neither can a corrupt tree bring forth good fruit. Every tree that bringeth not forth good fruit is hewn down and cast into the fire. Wherefore [because of the above facts] by their fruits ye shall know them."

The above Scriptures contain the key to knowing. We cannot improve upon the parable which Jesus chose to teach us about evil spirits and their fruit; so, let us take this comparison literally for a moment:

1. A wolf cannot produce the same fruit as a sheep.
2. He cannot grow wool.
3. He cannot be good food for the table.
4. He cannot follow the shepherd obediently like sheep; but, will lope around sniffing like the wolf that he is.
5. Even though he has a sheep skin on, he will not feed upon grass, as a sheep, but when he is hungry he will eat the sheep themselves.
6. He will "fleece" them. He will fool you for awhile, but he must produce fruit after his kind.

Jesus said so. Jesus is the Authority. He can tell us

13

about all of these things if we will just listen to Him!

A hunter is well aware of the fact that each animal must produce fruit after his kind, as each spirit must do. He knows what kind of animal he is following by his tracks and signs. No matter how well the sheep skin covered the wolf, his tracks could not be that of a sheep. He might try to bleat like a sheep, but when alone, he will howl like the wolf that he is. **So it is with the evil spirits.** You may not be sure whether a citrus tree is an orange, tangerine, lemon, lime, grapefruit, or kumquat, but you will be certain to know the name of it when you see the **fruit.** Jesus is saying it is the same with an evil spirit. An orange tree cannot bear a grapefruit. A spirit of jealousy **cannot** produce the fruit of a Deaf and Dumb spirit, etc.

Jesus did not say -- you would know them by comparing your impressions with the elders and asking if they witnessed to that person. No. Let me tell you, wolves in sheep's clothing make a career of meeting the right people and belonging to just the right church, and getting themselves accepted. This method is of the world and the world will receive them.

Except for the gifts, there is only one reliable method to try a spirit and that is the test given in Matthew 7:15-20. So...**HOW DO WE TRY A SPIRIT?**

Jesus told us that we would know them for certain by their **fruit.** I believe that the confusion of the Body of Christ is this: Jesus was definitely telling us how to try evil spirits whose abode is in the bodies of men. Instead of using it to know which evil spirits are working in a person by looking at the fruit, we have used this information to judge the brethren (human spirit) which we are not allowed to do.

It is obvious that we must study the Bible and find out the name of each spirit, and just what fruit that particular spirit produces. If we are to correctly try them, we must do it the Bible way. It takes work. It takes time.

14

Most of us are familiar with the fruit of the Holy Spirit. Most churches will agree that it is important to learn of this fruit. But how about the fruit of the evil spirits? I think it is even more important to know their fruit, and what each one produces, because the Holy Spirit will not hurt you. But, if you receive an evil spirit, he **will** hurt you. The Bible says satan comes but to steal, to kill, and to destroy. As Jesus said in Luke 9:55, not to be able to know what ''manner'' of spirit is manifesting, offends our Lord Jesus. Can you imagine how He must feel when you mistake an evil spirit for His Spirit?

Because we have not been taught the fruits of the principal spirits that are not of God, many of us did not know the correct way to try a spirit. But **now** we know the infallible method. The method that cannot fail...If we do it Jesus' way, we will not fail, nor will we be deceived. it will not be possible...

''Ye shall know them by their fruits.''

What if there are no manifestations or fruit? In trying a spirit, we either have the gift of Discerning of Spirits or -- ''watch 'em 'til they bear fruit,'' as spirits may be tried **only** by fruit. In the latter case, it would seem necessary to fellowship and give a spirit the benefit of the doubt until we have some evidential fruit by which we ''try the spirit'' whether it be of God or not.

The disadvantage in that is that by the time a tree begins to bear its fruit, we may find ourselves in quite a situation. We may find that there are many strongholds, fortresses and high things that the evil one has built up that must be pulled down. But seemingly worst of all for the sincere Christian is the blighted reputation one gets from the exposure or the association necessary to see the fruit produced.

If, after trial by fruit, you find you are dealing with an evil spirit, treat him like a demon -- resist, war, overcome, bind, and cast out. Do it aloud if convenient but, it is not necessary to do this aloud -- you do not need your mouth to wrestle a spirit. You need your mouth to teach the human spirit how to resist an evil spirit. You need your spirit and the Holy Spirit in a spirit to spirit battle. If you do this properly, you will free the human spirit from the evil spirit.

In the book, "How to Try a Spirit" I have assembled most of the principal strongmen for your convenience. I have listed much of the known **fruit** that the Bible teaches us that they bear, directly underneath the name. As Jesus said, it is an impossibility for one spirit to produce the same **fruit** of another spirit. You will never see this happen. For example, if in trying a spirit by its **fruit**, you should discover **fruit** belonging to another spirit, you have two spirits to deal with instead of one.

The Test

Jesus said grapes cannot be produced by a thorn bush -- a thorn bush must bring forth thorns...or figs from a briar. So likewise every spirit that does not bring forth true to its command by God to "bear fruit after its kind" is hewn down, and cast into the fire so that Jesus may present us with an infallible test; "wherefore by their fruits shall ye know them."

An example of trying the spirits by their fruit

You may be surprised at just how many of the Christian leaders and saints do not know how to try a spirit. I find myself amazed by such a lack of knowledge in the Body of Christ. I am going to give an example of just such an incident. I hope I can make it clear that this is not criticism, nor condemnation, but to hopefully instruct as to trying everything by the revealed Word of God.

I recently attended a meeting to hear an evangelist who is widely advertised and draws huge crowds. Before he began his ministry, he made this statement; "I am going to bind every demon that is in this building, and command that they go down the street while we are having this

16

meeting. Therefore, the only spirit that will operate in this auditorium will be the Holy Spirit.'' Then he proceeded to pray that prayer. Afterward, he told us that anything that we saw happening from henceforth would be ''of'' the Spirit of God.

Well...I thought...''let's try them and see''...After a short message, he called for all who had infirmities to come forward for healing.

What's wrong with that?

Shouldn't all those spirits of infirmities be down the street?

Surely those ugly things were not ''of God!'' the Bible classified spirits of infirmities as evil spirits. So, what fruit is manifesting in this man's statement: ''every spirit you see will be 'of God?'' I hear a Lying Spirit.

Two rows in front of me was a girl about ten years old. She was standing up swaying back and forth like a caged animal. Both hands were in her mouth; she was biting her fingers. She ran to the front for prayer every time he called for people to come forward. She needed deliverance. Her mother stuffed a handful of kleenex into her mouth to bite on instead of her fingers. Were all the demons gone?

How satan must have laughed! He was having a field day! He was handed the victory on many things without even a struggle. As far as the minister and many others were concerned, satan and all of his demons were down the street. Yes...satan had pulled off one of his best tricks, unhampered because of lack of knowledge. How pitiful. All of the knowledge needed to try the spirits was contained in the little black Bible the minister waved around in his hand. Although there were many pastors, and I am sure righteous men and women of God there, **no one** resisted satan! Why? Because the minister listened to a Lying Spirit and believed him. He then gave this lie to the people, and they were deceived by it.

17

"Beloved, believe not every spirit that comes to you, but try them whether they be of God or not. 1 John 4:1.

When the minister told the people they could believe every spirit they saw without testing, Satan had succeeded in catching believers off-guard and unaware. I did not believe him because his statement was in direct conflict with the revealed Word of God. I was inspecting **fruit**.

In the little girl, I saw torment, agitation, apprehension, nervous excitement, tension, and stress. She was hyperactive. all of these manifestations are the fruit of a demon of Fear. But, that was not the only one, she had two demons. Other fruit was being manifested.

She bit herself, gnashing her teeth, tearing at her body, bruising herself. The Dumb and Deaf spirit was compelling, driving her against her will to hurt herself. All of which is the fruit of the Dumb and Deaf demon.

I **know** them by their **fruit**. Those two demons never left the little girl to go down the street, as they were ordered. I know the **fruits** of the Holy Spirit, and that was not **Him**!

I saw the minister beckon to a young lady in the balcony. In a hypnotic trance, she arose and slowly made her way toward him. He backed his way across the stage, exhibiting his power over her to make her back up, stand still, or do whatever he commanded her in a hypnotic tone of voice. Then with screeching cries, the lady fell to the floor possessed with a demon.

She was "out in the spirit" they said. Out in the spirit? What spirit? Do we know the difference between God's Spirit and a Spirit of Divination? The Saints of the Most High God applauded, and the minister took a bow. I heard, "Praise the Lord! Amen!" As the people worshipped, the evil spirits exhibited their **fruit**.

I saw a man divining by a **Familiar Spirit**. How did I

know? By the **fruit**.

On page 41 of my book, **HOW TO TRY A SPIRIT**, is a list of the fruit that the **familiar spirit** and the **spirit of divination** produce.

I want to quote this scripture found in Deut. 19:8-12:

"Thou shalt not **LEARN TO DO** after the abominations of those nations. There shall not be found **AMONG YOU ANYONE**...that useth **DIVINATION**, or an observer of times, or an enchanter, or a witch, or a charmer, or a consulter with familiar spirits, or a wizard, or a necromancer. For **ALL** who do these things are an **ABOMINATION** unto the Lord!"

An abomination unto the Lord?... and the saints shouting "hallelujah and Praise ye the Lord?" They should have been resisting, and doing spiritual warfare. There is a time for praise, and a time for fighting. We must know when to do what. You do not applaud when evil spirits manifest, you fight.

You are going to have to learn to make distinctions between the Spirit of God, the human spirit, and the evil spirits.

1. **TRY THE SPIRIT:** If he is God - worship Him, obey Him, praise Him.
2. **TRY THE SPIRIT:** If he is unredeemed man - win him, loose him from the captivity of satan, and reconcile him to God!
3. **TRY THE SPIRIT:** If he is redeemed man - like the Bible says - encourage him, edify, strengthen him - love him, **even as** Jesus loves you.
4. **TRY THE SPIRIT:** If he is an angel - listen to him - receive him, co-operate with him, entertain him.
5. **TRY THE SPIRIT:** If it is satan - resist him and make him flee from you.

19

But, Beloved, receive not every spirit that comes to you as if they were ''of God'', but try them!...
BY THEIR FRUIT.

5
Wolves in Sheeps Clothing

"Beware of false prophets, which **come to you** in sheep's clothing, but inwardly they are ravening wolves."

You often pass signs that say, Madame so-and-so, fortune-teller, advisor, healer, etc. You know full well that this is not of God. And that she uses psychic power, and you will not likely **go to her**, or call upon the Familiar and Divining spirits that she has. But... you let that person put on a sheep's clothing and come to you... and to all apparent evidence she looks like a Christian. Will you believe her? Will you receive her? Or, will you recognize and know the wolf by its **fruit**?

It is important to know there are three kinds of power:
God Power
Satanic power
Psychic power

Those ministers who use psychic and satanic power to minister are usually those who want power but are unwilling to submit to the Holy Spirit, and be the clean, yielded vessel God requires. I believe that some of them start out with God, and then let sin come into their lives somewhere along the way. They then find themselves wrapped up in the programs of man. They find themselves standing in the pulpits, powerless. Hundreds of people are gathered to hear them. God will not anoint them because of sin in their lives. So with all eyes on them with expectation, they know they must "perform". The show must go on! They have their act all together. They have a reputation to live up to. They have to raise money. Now they must get into the flesh and "do" something, as any other actor would.

At this point, he is willing to "use divination" which simply means to do divine (or Godly) things by a Familiar Spirit!

I can see with my "spiritual eyes" exactly the way satan goes about to accomplish these defeats in the Body of Christ. He wishes to overthrow and seduce our top ministers. He does not bring them to this point overnight. No... he works in a subtle way. At the beginning he analyzes the situation, and plans his strategy.

Yes, satan has analyzed the minister and the situation. He knows the vulnerable spots to attack and that is where the attack will be launched. If one is watched long enough, these weaknesses could be easily spotted. We all have them. Satan gets this information before laying out his plan, and deciding which spirits will be used. If that minister is not "on guard", or doesn't know how to try a spirit and believes every spirit that comes to him to be "of God", he is easy prey. On the other hand, if he recognizes these human weaknesses in himself, and he knows a spirit by it's fruit, he will know that satan has set himself against him, not only to knock him out of action, but to actually use him. Then he will not be taken unaware, but will test, and resist that attack in the proper manner. Satan and his demons will flee from him. This is not to say they will give up. Not until they are chained or committed to the pit, will they cease to work.

Satan does not pull these ministers out of the ministry and put them in a witch coven, once they are in captivity. Oh no... he has deliberately allowed them to build up quite a reputation so that they will be well received by the Body of Christ. This is one of the reasons you cannot know them by checking out their background.

When satan has overthrown these ministers, he enslaves them to himself. You are a servant to whom you lend your members to. Now here is the part that is hard to understand. While this minister is performing or divining among the saints, who do not know how to try a spirit, many prayers of righteous men and women are going up to God in true faith, and they must avail much. **"The effectual fervent prayer of a righteous man availeth much** - Jas. 5:16.'' God is bound by His Word to honor them. Therefore miracles are actually taking place in the assembly while the fallen Minister is working. He is depending upon the righteous to pray the ''Prayer of Faith'' to save the sick. Isn't that sneaky? Yes.

Witches, Warlocks, and False Prophets need to do chants, charms, sacrifices, evil rites, and all manner of evil perverted works of the flesh to minister their evil. But praise God, we do the works of Jesus in Spirit and in Truth! Because of the blood sacrifice Jesus made once and for all, no ritual is necessary for believers to take authority over **ALL** the power of evil! Praise and honor and glory be to God for the unspeakable gift of His Son, Jesus Christ! Here is what should be done when faced with this situation: After you have tried the spirit and found it not to be of God, do not wish the minister Godspeed in any way by taking an active part. Do not join in the worship, or pray.

11 Jn. 7-11 - shows how we can become a partaker with these antichrist spirits. Look at verse 11. We actually become a partaker if we participate in the meeting. If you do not know how to war and do battle... then walk out!

Realize that even though those in the audience are silent, it is still possible to do many healings, deliverances, or whatever the need may be. Since we wrestle not with flesh and blood we do not need our mouth, arms, legs, etc. to work in the spirit realm.

Jesus said, ''Behold, I send you forth as sheep in the mist of wolves: (Wolves are a symbol of false prophets) be ye therefore wise as serpents, (serpents are wise enough not to unduly expose themselves to unnecessary attack, likewise a Christian should be wise enough to recognize the wolf, and be harmless as doves (doves never provoke

23

enmity) - Mt. 10:16. What a wise example Jesus chose to teach us this truth! Clear distinction must be drawn between the human spirit, and the evil spirit. To the human spirit you should send forth the Spirit of Supplication and Grace to plead with him that he may be made aware of his position and sin; that he remember the price Jesus paid at Calvery; that perhaps he might be brought to repentance.

On the other hand, launch a powerful counter attack against the evil spirits. Aim these weapons of God directly at the enemy. They are mighty to pulling down every stronghold, and nullifying every clever and crafty tactic. Overpower them with that Spirit in you that is greater than all those that are in the world.

**LET GOD THE HOLY GHOST ARISE
AND HIS ENEMIES WILL BE SCATTERED!**

6
Casting Out Devils

Did you know that Jesus Himself classified the casting out of devils as the Gift of "Working of Miracles?" He did not say those who cast them out had a deliverance ministry. Any time you confront a person all bound up with an evil spirit, and by the finger of God throw the spirit out, and take that person for Jesus, you have worked a miracle! Not only that, but you are working the works of God!

Let us take a look at our Scriptures that prove casting out devils is the "Working of Miracles."

Mark 9:38, "**And John answered him, saying, Master, we saw one CASTING OUT DEVILS in thy name, and he followeth not us; and we forbade him, because he followeth not us.**" Listen to the way Jesus answered John, Mark 9:39, "**But Jesus said, Forbid him not; for there is no man which shall DO A MIRACLE IN MY NAME, that can speak evil of me.**"

Jesus said **casting out a devil was doing a miracle!**

Acts 8:6, "**And the people with one accord gave heed unto those things which Philip spake, hearing and seeing the MIRACLES which he did.**" What miracles? Casting out devils.

Acts 8:7 "**For unclean spirits, crying with loud voices came out of many that were possessed with them: and many taken with palsies, and that were lame, were healed.** (The Bible is saying all these things are caused by devils...)

Listen, Pastor, how can you stand in your pulpit looking out into faces of wretched people who are all bound up by

25

devils, and refuse to cast them out?

Is it because you are afraid someone will misunderstand? It is the lack of power in the Church that people do not understand. Where will they go for help?

CAST OUT A DEVIL... the news of it will quickly spread abroad. Your building will fill up with people who want to see a miracle. Then you will have many people to minister to. These miracles are the signs Jesus gave.

Scream out from your pulpits loud and clear, "The Kingdom of God has come nigh unto you!" Every devil in hell will shudder. And no one will sleep through your sermon.

Look through the New Testament. See that Jesus told His followers to go and say that the Kingdom of Heaven is at hand. Then when they had everyone's attention, told them about the Kingdom. (Matt. 10:7,8.) Then show them about it by casting out devils, healing the sick, or whatever the need may be.

If you say you are a minister of God, then minister His goods! Many who say they do not believe in deliverance, do believe, however, in the gifts of the Spirit and would be happy to do a miracle.

Denominations who shun the casting out of devils are banning two important gifts of the Holy Ghost from their midst... the working of miracles and discerning of spirits. That mistake stems from a stiff-necked attitude that Jesus certainly did not have when dealing with devils openly.

The word Christian means to be Christ-like in every way: to follow and imitate His example and His commands. If He practiced it, then it is good enough for us. Jesus of Nazareth went about doing good!

I have had some say to me that they did not agree with my theology on deliverance from demons. It is not my

Theology at all. It is the Son of God's.

JESUS IS HIS NAME:

It isn't that we choose to do deliverance, but we are commanded to do it! It isn't optional at all. It is simply to obey what you are told to do.

The work that He called us to do is to believe God, that we might meet the needs of individuals. This work includes ''letting the oppressed go free of evil spirits.''

This was the kind of ministry Jesus had, and it was a well balanced one. I consider a ministry which refuses to deal with Satan, an unbalanced one. Jesus did, and taught His disciples, to deal with the powers of darkness as they are the primary cause of sin and sickness in this world.

I have never understood how someone could minister to sickness and not believe in deliverance from evil spirits, for a **SPIRIT OF INFIRMITY** is causing the sickness, and must be bound before his goods are destroyed. Otherwise, he may produce more goods.

Much of Jesus' ministry was directed against devils. On the one hand He bound the strongman, while on the other hand He destroyed his goods.

Ministers of God need to be aggressive against the cause of the problems, using mighty weapons of God to destroy the works of Satan. Jesus' work included conquering Satan by His death; delivering people out of Satan's captivity. Should our work be any less? Jesus said it should be greater.

As one brother so aptly put it, ''Deliverance is not an extra addition to the preaching of the Gospel, it is the very **CENTER** of the Gospel itself.''

Jesus came into the world for the express purpose to set the captives free, and to set at naught the works of the Devil and his demons. (1 John 3:8; Isa. 61:1; Acts 10:38.)

I thank God for deliverance.

My dander gets up when I hear that those of us who are faithful to cast out demons, are referred to as "demon Chasers." I say it is better to chase them than to run from them like the sons of Sceva did! Resist the Devil and he will flee from you. Some of us act as if **we** are the flee-ee, instead of Satan. No, we are more than conquerors, not the conquered! That is Satan's part. (the defeated foe.)

The very reason people don't understand is because there has not been enough of it done in the open. The spirits being subject to us, is one of the signs following believers. It also causes unbelievers to believe!!Miracles of deliverance are seen to be a seal attending God's divine authority. Don't tell me **that** should be done in private!

I don't find one case in my Bible where they sneaked behind a building to cast out a demon. I say let the discreet hide in the closet, let us cast out demons as Jesus did. Let them go out screaming, yelling, and gnashing of teeth!

Binding and Loosing are the Keys to the Kingdom

"And I will give unto thee the keys of the Kingdom of Heaven; and WHATSOEVER thou shalt bind on earth shall be bound in Heaven; and WHATSOEVER thou shalt loose on earth shall be loosed in Heaven. Again I say unto you, WHATSOEVER ye shall bind on earth shall be bound in Heaven; and WHATSOEVER ye shall loose on earth shall be loosed in Heaven." Matt. 16:19; Matt. 18:18.

7
By What Authority?

Spiritual authority is knowing who you are in Christ Jesus. It is knowing your correct relationship to the Father and the Son, Jesus Christ. It is knowing just what position you are in. It is in knowing what is yours, to have and to hold. All that which was wrought upon Calvary and delivered unto the Saints, is yours, and more. It is in knowing what is expected of you -- what part you are to have in the Eternal Kingdom -- your responsibility toward God. His part -- your part.

I could not cast out a demon until I knew beyond a doubt that I was supposed to do it; until I searched the Scriptures and found out demons were subject to obey me, and that I had authority over them, because without God-given dominion, man wrestles with unconquerable forces.

I could not receive a healing for myself or others until I established the truth in my own mind that healing is the children's bread! It was this knowledge, written in Holy Scriptures, that enabled me to pray the prayer of faith that would heal the sick.

When I found out that God commanded me to; preach, fast, let the oppressed go free, undo heavy burdens, cast out demons, heal the sick, etc., I could then obey Him. I knew He had empowered me, through the Holy Ghost, for this work.

Spiritual authority is seeing the whole picture **now**, and walking in the light of **knowing**. It is in rising above the circumstances that we are able to exercise spiritual authority. Without spiritual authority one can become bogged down in confusion and fog without the understanding of why. I am going to try to give you an overall picture proving that we are given authority.

A picture of God... Daniel 7:9-11.

"I beheld till the thrones were cast down, and the Ancient of Days did sit, whose garment was white as snow, and the hair of His head like the pure wool; His throne was like the fiery flame, and His wheels as burning fire. A fiery stream issued and came forth from before Him: thousand thousands ministered unto Him, and ten thousand times ten thousand stood before Him; the judgment was set, and the books were opened. I beheld then because of the voice of the great words which the horn spake: I beheld even till the beast was slain, and his body destroyed, and given to the burning flame..."

A picture of Christ... Daniel 7:13, 14.

"I saw in the night visions, and behold, One like the Son of man came with the clouds of heaven, and came to the Ancient of Days, and they brought Him near before Him. And there was given Him dominion, and glory, and a kingdom, that all people, nations, and languages, should serve Him; His dominion is an everlasting dominion, which shall not pass away, and His Kingdom that which shall not be destroyed."

A picture of you... Daniel 7:18, 21, 22, 27.

"But the saints of the most High shall take the Kingdom, and possess the Kingdom forever, even forever and ever. I beheld, and the same horn made war with the saints, and prevailed against them; Until the Ancient of Days came, and judgment was given to the saints of the Most High; and the time came that the saints possessed the Kingdom. And the Kingdoms and dominions,

**and the greatness of the Kingdom under the
whole Heaven, shall be given to the people of the
saints of the Most High, whose Kingdom is an
everlasting Kingdom, and all dominions shall
serve and obey Him.''**

Our ultimate calling is to be kings and priests unto
Jesus, and unto His Father.

Revelations 1:5, 6... **And from Jesus Christ,
who is the faithful witness, and the first Begotten
of the dead, and the Prince of the kings of the
earth. Unto Him that loved us, and washed us
from our sins in His Own Blood. And hath made
us KINGS AND PRIESTS unto God and His
Father; to Him be glory and dominion forever and
ever. Amen.**

Romans 8:17... **Joint-heirs, partnership. He,
the Head, we the body.**

Now that we have established our position, I have a
question for you. Will we become rulers over the
governments of the world with **no** training? No, we will not!

Prince Charles of England, at a certain age, entered into
a planned, disciplined program of studies and work that are
designed to prepare him for his rulership as the King of
England. (a.) The earthly way is to raise a crown prince to
be a king. (b.) God's method also is to put His elect through
a rigid training program that will prepare them to
administer God's will over the whole earth. What a marvel
that every person born into the family of God is born into
royalty! Yes, Divine Royalty! Colossians 1:13 declares, **''He
hath translated us into the Kingdom of His Dear Son.''**
Being born into the Royal Family gives you the right to use
the Divine Name -- Jesus Christ!

''Make level in the desert a highway for our God.'' By
the message we are to bear and the comfort He enjoins us
to give, we actually are in the process of making level in the

dry, dry desert, a highway for our God. If we could only realize it, we are in the **preparation** state of our ministry as God's messengers. I believe that our service to God in the ages to come, is -- being determined largely by the manner in which we **exercise** our ministry before Him now.

Please read the above statement again and again. It is of the utmost importance to **know**.

"Those who do not know Christ should realize that death does not end all... 'It is appointed unto men ONCE TO DIE and after this cometh judgment.' Heb. 9:27. Christians, too, need to be aware that death does not end our service to Him. (The devil uses this idea to make you passive.) We are to continue as servants of Jehovah throughout the eternal ages, reigning with Him and serving Him forever and ever, and **we are being prepared** for that service right here and now." How?

What is the purpose of it all? For quite some time now the question, "For what purpose?", has presented itself to me. My quest to understand the purpose of God in my life has ended in wisdom from above. I have found the answer! What is the answer? I am sure that the kings would not be willing to go through such rigid training if he were only a rich individual. But he is aware that those things for which he is giving up his personal life, are to prepare him for his ultimate rule as king. Are you aware of this fact? Wouldn't the testing trials that purify us be easier if we too understood the purpose?

The Spirit itself beareth witness with our spirit, that we are the children of God: And if children, then heirs; heirs of God, and joint-heirs with Christ; if so be that we suffer with Him, that we may be also glorified together. Answer: the saints are going to share the glory! ALL RIGHT! **For I reckon that the sufferings of this present time are not worthy to be compared with the glory which shall be revealed IN US** -- Romans 8:16-18.

32

We know from studying the Scriptures on the Kingdom of God that we are to rule well over His earthly household and the goods that He delivered unto us when He went away. Let us take a look at that picture: Matthew 25:14, 21, 23, 31, 34, KJV. Christ's goods have been delivered to us already, and if we rule well over these things, He will put us over many.

The definition of rule is: to govern, control, direct, manage, command, decree, have complete dominion in His stead, doing His Word and work with his commission and the authority of His **now**!

Realize how necessary it is for you to rule over these things in your life, such as exercising authority over evil spirits, commanding them in the Name of Jesus with a Rod of Iron. Rev. 2:27.

God has big plans for us! He has us in a school of intensive training by the Holy Ghost Himself. It is a program designed to condition us to our high call. The program for Prince Charles has been ordered by Queen Elizabeth and the wisdom of the royal kings that ruled before her down through the ages. Our training has been ordered by the King over all kings. It is our Father's good pleasure to give us the Kingdom. This world belongs to **our** Father, and the fullness thereof.

> Daniel 7:18: **"But in the end the people of the Most High God shall rule the governments of the world forever and ever."**
>
> Verse 21......**"For I had seen this horn warring against God's people and winning."**
>
> Verse 22......**"Until the Ancient of Days came and opened His court and vindicated His people, giving them worldwide powers of government."**

33

Verse 27......"Then every nation under
Heaven, and all their power,
shall be given to the people of
of God; they shall rule all things
forever, and ALL RULERS shall
serve and obey Him." We will be
ruling ALL Kings!

These things that Jesus delivered unto us to rule over
now is only a fraction of what we will inherit in the
everlasting Kindgom of our God.

So, friends, let us enter into this ministry with
submission to God -- preparing ourselves to be fit vessels
for this high calling in Christ Jesus!

8
Fight a Good Fight
Conduct Spiritual Warfare!

It is important for every born again person to realize that he is involved in a contest with the enemy; and that he will never reach his goals to attain the spiritual progress, the crowns, the prize of the high callings that are in Christ Jesus without a tremendous struggle. **"Shall your brethren go to war, and shall ye SIT here?"** Numbers 32:68.

If you intend to be one of those who **sit** on the fence, or stay neutral, or never wrestle with the powers and principalities in the air over Blood bought victories, you probably will never hear those words from Jesus: "Well done, my good and faithful servant!" If you are busy withstanding those who **are** wrestling and casting out devils, you may hear the words, "Depart from me, ye workers of iniquity!"

Many would like to accept only the love, the rewards, the goodies of God, and leave the fighting of the battles, the wrestling, to the others. But not so! You may get by without fighting if you wish. But those evil spirits are not playing games with you. They are going to fight. If you want to give up without resistance, go ahead and surrender unconditionally. They will gladly take you into captivity. They will enslave you and use you at their will. But this is not the way of the Lord. He said **RESIST** the devil and give him no place. He said **HE** gave you power over them. But it is surely up to you to **use** it.

We are already in a period of terrible warfare. Terrible, because we are fighting unseen forces. Terrible, because, we, for the most part, are unprepared to war in the spiritual realm. Terrible, because, in spite of the training God has set up, many Christians are shirking their responsibility to make the necessary efforts to prepare themselves for war. What will be the results? Many will not finish their course. They will be defeated. Many of God's very elect will be deceived by evil spirits. (1 Tim. 4:1,2)

What I am saying to you, Beloved, is: Whether you fight or not is not your choice. War has been declared. How much you know about fighting the battle will decide which way the battle goes! Every single conflict that comes your way is a chance for you to win a victory over the devil.

The battle of the ages is on!

The battle truly is fought out in the soul of man. Control of the thoughts, emotions, will, and faith are the objectives or prizes that are being fought for.

No country ever goes to war without finding out who they are declaring war upon, and what the objective is. Yet some of us blindly relinquish the faith that was once delivered to us by Jesus' Blood-bought victory on Calvary, without so much as a good struggle! It is not pleasing to Christ Jesus for us to give up at the onset of the battle, nor at all! Those that **overcome** to the end will have rewards.

Paul demonstrated the power of God along the course of his journey. Those that withstood the Gospel, asserting themselves against Paul and Peter were led away blind or carried out dead! This may seem a bit harsh to you...but this is the way of war. It is not a Sunday picnic. Wars are won by...
> force,
>> strength,
>>> resistance,
>>>> power...

The enemy is come to kill, steal, maim, and destroy. If we do not fight and win, they will accomplish their mission upon us!

Paul was a soldier of the Cross of Jesus Christ. So are

we, or we should be. Paul knew how to fight a good fight. First, in the flesh before he was apprehended by Jesus Christ. He persecuted, threatened, and imprisoned many disciples of Christ. He warred such a good war against Christians that Christ said to him, "Saul, Saul, why are you persecuting Me?" Now...that's what I call some kind of fighter! After Jesus Christ overthrew Paul on the road to Damascus, Paul then excelled in Spiritual warfare. Now he fought for a different Master...he defected to the other side.

Before his conversion, **Paul had authority from the chief priest** to bind all that **called on** the Name of Jesus. **After** his conversion to Jesus Christ, he had **authority from The Chief Priest [Jesus]** to bind all that **opposed** that Name.

Paul declared that he fought a good fight...and indeed he did!

What kind of fight are we putting up? Puny! In some cases...pitiful! Most certainly not fit to offer to the Master!

A good warrior is one that is able in any arena, or any kind of struggle with the enemy to war a splendid warfare...a victory over the enemy...one that is fit for our Lord Jesus Christ. A victory that will get a "well done" from the Lord.

Our aim as a soldier is to satisfy the One who enlisted us, that is, Christ.

The Pauline Revelations reveal that Paul fought to win. In 1 Corinthians 9:26, he said that he did not fight as one **beating the air**. Not as one uncertain, but that he fought with a purpose...to win!

How often I see my brethren **beat the air**. They don't bother to find out who they are fighting or where the enemy is attacking. Can you imagine the President of the United States after the attack on Pearl Harbor, not bothering to find out who to launch a counter attack against? Or, perhaps declaring war on France instead of Japan? Beating the air, as one uncertain. Wouldn't victory be more certain if we learned about our enemy...his position...his strength...and how to defeat him? Had the United States had the proper information when Pearl Harbor was attacked, had they resisted properly, perhaps we would not have lost so much of our Navy.

One of the first principles of war is: To locate and identify the enemy.

Who is the enemy?

"For WE wrestle not against flesh and blood [persons] but against principalities, against powers, against the rulers of the darkness of this world, against spiritual wickedness in high places," Eph. 6:12.

Notice that **we** are the ones expected to wrestle. We are not fighting people made of flesh and blood, but against unseen persons without bodies...great evil princes...huge numbers of evil spirits. We are fighting principalities...rulers, leaders, executives, chiefs, heads, masterminds, controllers, and main strongmen. We are fighting against their powers... Eph. 6:10,11...Wiles, tricks, strategy, craftiness, cunning; We are fighting against their skills, their deceitfulness, their devices, their schemes, or contrivances.

We are told in 11 Corinthians 2:11 that we are not to be ignorant of these devices, lest satan get an advantage over us. It is to our advantage to correctly know, who, how many, their individual power, what they do, and what area is under attack.

We should not be as concerned with common demons as we are with these strongmen. They are assigned over all dark works in this world. We are to fight against wickedness in high places. There is a principal force behind every dark work whom our battle is with. Do not bother to launch a battle against a certain sin or work (fruit). Even if you were successful in your attack, you would not have touched the main source. He would be free to work elsewhere. For example, do not launch your attack against the fruit, goods, or manifestation, but as Christ said, **the strongman**, and secondly spoil his goods -- Matt. 12:29, 30.

These principals under Lucifer's command are those who wage war on the saints of God. They will try to wear down the saints! They will not have mercy upon us, they will use **all** their power and strength against us. They also fight with a purpose...to win. Neither do they fight as one beating the air!

Who is the enemy?

In addition to the principal strongmen spirits listed in the book, **How to Try a Spirit**, there are the living wicked spirits who have rejected Christ and chosen Satan. These are **not** the possessed nor bound, therefore are not in need of deliverance. **Their human spirits** are the actual strongmen that must be bound and dealt with by the Believers. Because **they** are high ranking principal forces in the satanic kingdom. They control and direct demons. These are called Witches, Mediums, Fortune Tellers, Psychics, Magicians, and Sorcerers.

Let us look for example, at the Apostle Paul in order to learn how he dealt with such an enemy, Acts 13: 6-12.

Verse 6 and 7, Barnabas and Paul had just been separated and sent out by the Holy Ghost when they met Barjesus, whose name was also Elymas the sorcerer. He was with the **"deputy of the country, Sergius Paulus, a prudent man; who called for Barnabas and Saul, and desired to hear the Word of God."**

Verse 8, **"But Elymas the sorcerer [for so is his name by interpretation] WITHSTOOD them, seeking to turn away the deputy from the faith."**

Here we have a spiritual war over faith. How did Paul fight it?

Verse 9, 10, "**Then, Saul, [who also is called Paul,] filled with the Holy Ghost, set his eyes on him, And said, O full of all subtilty and all mischief, thou child of the devil, thou enemy of all righteousness, wilt thou not cease to pervert the right ways of the Lord?''**

Paul did not pat him on the back and try to win Elymas the sorcerer to the Lord; he didn't begin to sing praises; he didn't turn the other cheek; he quickly located and identified him as **the enemy.** Then he exercised the power and authority delegated to him, (Eph. 1:20-22 and 2:6.) He **judged.** We cannot judge the brethren, but we can judge devils! He tried the spirit, found it evil and treated it like a devil. Here is his judgment:

Verse 11, "**And now, behold, the hand of the Lord is upon thee, and thou shalt be blind, not seeing the sun for a season.''**

Then what? God backed his words with power from on high! "**And immediately there fell on him a mist and a darkness; and he went about seeking some to lead him by the hand.''**

We need this same power of God to be demonstrated in **our** lives for the bringing in of the Kingdom.

Verse 12, "**Then the deputy, when he saw what was done, believed, being astonished at the doctrine of the Lord.''**

- The deputy was astonished.
- We need to **astound** more people.
- To astonish: (Webster) to make thunder-struck.
- To strike or impress with wonder, or admiration,
- To surprise,

amaze, stun,

shock, to confound.

40

It is going to take more in this day of sorcery and all out open warfare, than to make a measley little sermonette called "Jesus loves you, anyhow!" Jesus hates the low down way most of us are, and wants us to walk in His deliverance from it! We need to do as the church at Antioch was doing when the Holy Ghost said, "Separate me Barnabas and Saul for the work whereunto I have called them. (You mean the Holy Ghost called them to go and blind Elymas?) You got it. (Acts 13:2). But Christians are only supposed to do good! That **was** good. Yes, we need to come together, minister to the Lord, fast and pray until we hear from Heaven. We need something more than drumming up a spiritual high by stamping our feet, clapping our hands, putting our arms around the person sitting next to us, and saying, "Jesus loves you." We need to speak with such power and demonstration of the Spirit of God that they rise up and gnash us with their teeth, as Stephen, they become so enraged! Beloved, we need this kind of astonishment to convince the people that God Almighty is backing us as we go.

The deputy was **astonished.** At what? The **doctrine** of the Lord! You mean to tell me that blinding someone could be part of the doctrine of Christ? I thought Jesus only did good. That **was** good, righteous, and the right way to fight the devil and win!

Paul said Fight -- Wrestle -- War...

1 Timothy 6:12: **Fight the good fight of faith, lay hold on eternal life, whereunto thou art also called, and hast professed a good profession before many witnesses.''**

You know, Brother Paul did not mince any words when it came to warning the enemy! He sent word to them not to think of him as though he were a mere man walking in the flesh! That he might walk in the flesh, but he certainly did not fight like a human being! Not even with human weapons. He informed them that the weapons he intended to use against them were not those men had made such as

41

clubs, spears, swords, darts, arrows, etc., but mighty weapons of God! He told them he hoped he wouldn't need to show them how harsh and rough he could be, and that he really did not wish to carry out his present plan of attack against them, for he was no ordinary weak human being as he may appear to be in the physical. He threatened that the plans and methods he used to win his battles were not human. They were supernatural weapons belonging to Almighty God, Himself!

WOW! I most certainly would not want to come up against an enemy like Brother Paul, would you? Those evil Corinthians must have been shaking in their boots. Every demon in them must have fled in terror before he arrived!! Could it be that we are too mealy-mouthed when it comes to using our authority in Jesus' Name?

Paul said that he could bring these powerful, mighty weapons against them and:

1. Break down every proud argument against God.
2. Knock down every wall that can be built to keep men from finding God.
3. Capture every backslider or person who is rebelling against God's way and order, and bring them back to God, and make them like it!
4. Change them into men whose heart's desire is obedience to Christ!
5. Pull down mighty forces and strongholds they had built up.
6. Put to flight all the demon powers and alien armies in existence!
7. Subdue all the boasted gods and systems that exalt themselves against the knowledge of God -- the Gospel he preached.
11 Cor. 10:2—16, **THE LIVING BIBLE.**

Paul told the leaders of the church that he intended to use these weapons against every rebel who remained after he first used them against the leaders themselves and **made** them surrender to Christ.

Now, I ask you -- Is that a fair way to fight? Well, nevertheless, he went on terrorizing them and said: "The trouble with you folks is you think I am just boasting about my claim of authority over you, but when I get there my personal presence is going to be as rough on you as my letters." He said that he had **all of God's power** to use in dealing them them! II Cor. 13:4, LB

Wouldn't these weapons help us with our warfare? Let us find out what they are and use them.

What are these powerful, mighty weapons of God?

Without God given **dominion** we are fighting unconquerable forces! But, He has given us:

1. **His** dominion over all evil forces -- "the spirits are subject to you." They must mind every word you say. If spirits are not minding you...you probably are not giving them many orders! We are supposed to be telling them what to do, and where to go. With God given dominion, the devil and **all** his forces are fighting **unconquerable** forces! When Jesus ascended, He gave gifts to men. He prayed to the Father, and the Father gave us:
2. **HIS SPIRIT**, the same spirit that Jesus used when He delivered the demoniac!! **WHEN JESUS LEFT, HE GAVE US:**
3. **HIS NAME** to use. He said, "In My Name ye shall preach, cast out devils and heal the sick, cleanse the lepers, and raise the dead. Before Jesus left He gave Us;
4. **HIS BLOOD** -- shed for the remission of sins -- justifying us in the sight of God. Through that Blood we can come into God's

presence. (See Chap. 15)

1. submit ourselves to God.
2. resist the devil with confidence that he
3. is going to flee!

Because in such a state as that, we are too much, too many, and too powerful for the devil.

With God given dominion the devil and all of his spirits are fighting against unconquerable forces!

The fact is we are marvelously equipped for the struggle.

More than conquerors!

He gave:

5. **HIS STRENGTH:** "You can do **all things** through Christ who strengthens you." Without Him, we can do nothing, but with Him there is nothing we cannot do.
6. **HIS WORD:** We speak the **WORD**, quote it, and it shall go **forth** and accomplish what we send it to do!

"Unto **you** a Son is given." Unto us? Yes, we **have** Jesus -- **all** that He is and was!

WE HAVE:

1. His Name	8. His Knowledge	15. His Might
2. His Flesh	9. His Strength	16. His Armour
3. His Spirit	10. His Dominion	17. His Work
4. His Blood	11. His Word	18. His Image
5. His Life	12. His Power	19. His Stead
6. His Mind	13. His Joy	20. His Reward
7. His Wisdom	14. His Counsel	21. His Inheritance

and HIM and HIS FATHER and THE KINGDOM!
IS THERE ANYTHING ELSE?

9
Keep the Faith

What are we fighting over: Jude 3b, **"and exhort you that ye should earnestly contend for the FAITH."**

These powers of darkness are fighting to overthrow our **faith**...to dilute, to debate it, to divert, to overthrow it, to convince us, if possible, to the contrary. Paul said **FIGHT, WRESTLE, WAR.**

"Fight the good fight of faith, lay hold on eternal life, whereunto thou art also called, and has professed a good profession before many witnessess" — 1 Tim. 6:12.

Know what God said and believe and obey Him, regardless of how impossible or foolish it may appear to others. Agree with Him that His estimation of all the situations on which He speaks are true estimations. For God wants man to know that **He** is faithful to His Word, watching over it to see that every Word is performed and everything it is sent to do is accomplished. And...that He meant exactly what He said. Reject and cast off all that is contrary to that Word.

Why are we fighting over faith?

Because...through faith we:
(Heb. 11:33, 34)

1. Subdue kingdoms (kingdom of darkness.)
2. Wrought righteousness (make the right way of the Lord reign.)
3. Obtain promises (appropriate the benefits and powers of the Kingdom of God, execute

45

God's laws to the letter.)
4. Stop the mouths of lions (stop the lies of devils, lock the jaws of liars, tread on and take dominion over devils.)
5. Quench the violence of fire (as the Hebrew children, neither scorched nor burned.)
6. Escape the edge of the sword (no weapon formed against you will prosper, Isaiah 54:17)
7. Are made strong.
8. Wax valiant in fight (against the enemy.)
9. Turn to flight the armies of the aliens.

If the enemy can test, try and overthrow your faith, he can stop you from doing all of these things!

Over the Faith

What Is Faith?

1. Strict adherence to the Word of God.
   a. Adhesion, stick fast, glued to, unmovable in spite of any contrary evidence to the promises, doctrines, covenants,
   b. A firm belief to the point of total trust in the covenant maker--**GOD**!

2. Recognition of spiritual realities and principles as supreme.
   a. The highest in authority or power.
   b. The everlasting truth or fact that one may rely on in spite of any other principle, authority, document, doctrine, medical, science, etc.

3. Fidelity, loyalty, careful observance, exact, accurate.
   a. True in allegiance as a subject or bondslave to our Sovereign, Lord, and King.
   b. A servant worthy of the Sovereign's

confidence that the subject will not be:
        fickle
                wavering
                        swayed to another
                                disloyal to the
                                        MASTER...

Keep the Faith

What the Word says about healing, deliverance, eternal life, etc. When the Spirit of Infirmity attacks faith, divine healing is the issue; the prize or benefit that Satan desires to take away is the right to be healed by His stripes. Each time that the enemy engages you in a spiritual conflict, try the spirit by the fruit produced. Know who you are fighting. Ask yourself what the objective is. Every time, dear brethren, the objective will be to overthrow the **FAITH** on a particular doctrinal issue.

Are you going to be able to say as Paul did in 11 Tim. 4: 7, 8, **"I have fought a good fight, I have finished my course, I have kept the FAITH? Henceforth there is laid up for me a crown of righteousness, which the Lord, the righteous Judge, shall give me at that day; and not to me only, but unto all them also that love His appearing."**

Have Faith In God!

Ye have been given power,
    to preach, heal, cast out devils,
    and raise the dead.
To disappear in a riot,
    walk on water,
    and feed the multitude
    without bread.
If ye have faith of a mustard seed;
    ye can pull up a tree, as if it were a weed.
    Remove a mountain,
    and plant it in the sea,
Ye have only to believe,
    IN ME.
How long will I be with you
    to teach and to train?
Listen closely now,
    while I show you again.
Remember the loaves and the fishes,
    and try your best to understand
That our work does not depend,
    upon the laws of nature,
    nor, the laws of man!
How long will ye suffer me,
    before ye will know?
I AM THE SON OF GOD,
    for I have told you so.

by Mary Garrison

48

10
Satan and His Demons are the Flee-e... Not We!

1. Submit yourself to God
2. Resist the Devil,
   and he will flee from you.

When we go into the Holy of Holiest, (see Chap. 15), we submit ourselves to God. From that lofty position, put on our whole armour, (Eph 6), take up our mighty weapons, (Chap 8), put on faith (Chap 9), turn and resist the devil, **the** only recourse left for the devils is to flee, run, retreat, unconditionally surrender, or be captured and punished.

Be alert -- pay close attention to what is happening, what is being said, the thoughts you are getting, the events, what is actually coming to pass (the facts, what is being threatened or could happen. By being knowledgeable and on guard, we can be victorious in our lives and those that come to our attention. We do not have to tolerate nor allow an evil spirit to work unhindered. We are to test him by his fruit, bind him, cast him out of our territory, then set about destroying his goods. Once this is done we are to work on these areas ourselves producing the fruits of righteousness that **will** remain. Remember, this is not flesh and blood work, not carnal, but spiritual. The demons do not get permission to entice, seduce, and deceive. Neither did I read where Jesus asked the victim if he wanted Him to deliver him. I see he dealt with them wherever they crossed His path! He instructed us to take the same dominion over them. They have **no** rights. We have **every** right as those human bodies and souls belong to our Father. We do not have to tolerate them. We can **dismiss** them.

49

11
Seducing Spirit

"Now the Spirit speaketh expressly, that in the latter times some shall depart from the faith, giving heed to seducing spirits, and doctrines of devils; Speaking lies in hypocrisy; having their conscience seared with a hot iron." 11 tim. 4:1

Manifestations (fruit) of the seducing spirit;

Sear the conscience
Seduce
Entice
Tempt
Allure
Excite
Interest
Fascinate
Attract
Arouse
Win Over
To bring in a deceiving spirit.

A Seducing spirit is an evil Emissary sent from Satan to perform a certain Mission. That mission is to overthrow a particular person, taking him into captivity. Having accomplished that task, he then turns his victim over to another spirit to do **his** particular job upon that person. The next spirit may be any number of evil spirits: Deceiving, Lying Perverse, etc. We could say the Seducing spirit is a "fore-runner" for many others. He must accomplish his task before many others can start, as each spirit **must** bear fruit after his kind, so that we can try them by their fruit. Jesus said so! The Seducing spirit is only responsible for the initial work of seduction. His purpose is to: sear the conscience, seduce, tempt, allure, excite, interest, fascinate, attract, arouse, and win over and bring in another spirit.

1. The **seducing spirit** will carefully select the yielded vessel (person) he has chosen to work through. This decision will be based upon the particular weakness of the victim -- lust, etc. He will work untiringly, unceasingly upon these weak areas in the victim until he surrenders without further resistance. It is only after the victim has given heed, (pay attention -- given place to ---- listened with interest to), that the Seducing spirit can inflict his next blow!

2. Now what? The Seducing spirit knows that the person (victim), and every man, has within him the ability to know the right way, and to know God. This knowledge of God is seated in a part of the body we call conscience. The Seducing spirit now moves in for a paralyzing blow to the conscience. He burns or sears the conscience, the Bible says, as if with a hot iron. The dictionary says: To cauterize it, to make callous, withered, hardened, and insensible to distinquish between right and wrong. The Seducing spirit renders the conscience unable to actively and alertly rebuke, condemn, and effectively resist the dark force used by this demon.

Now the victim has a terrible wound -- or burn -- a burn is very susceptible to germs of all kinds. There is no resistance in a burned area.

Now that there is no ability left in the victim to divide right from wrong, he is in total submission to the evil spirit. The job of the Seducing spirit is coming to an end in the victim. He will then lead the victim astray into error, turning him over to whichever demon is to carry on. Then a

Deceiving, Perverse, etc., will begin to minister to him. We may try the incoming spirit by its fruit -- so as to know the name.

But take heed to yourselves

Christians are noted for their gullibility. But this is not the way Jesus has instructed us to be. A demon has tried to teach us to be easily tricked, cheated, or defrauded. Jesus took great care to warn us of this. Saying, "Take heed; behold, I have foretold you all things." And He did! We just don't always bother to seek them out properly.

Seven ways to avoid seduction:

1. Regard with care.
2. Pay close attention.
3. Notice what fruit is being produced.
4. Observe carefully, rightly dividing the truth.
5. Use presence of mind.
6. Do not be foolish.
7. Try the spirits, whether they be of God.

How are we to loose those who are seduced?

1. Bind the strongman demons, calling them by the proper name.
2. The Seducing Spirit must be ousted from both bodies, the seducer and seduced which he lives and operates through. He must be commanded not to come back.

Now we are stuck with **all** the damage done -- his goods. We still have a deceived victim, a messed-up life, perhaps a head full of error, a smashed-up home -- separated family, habits built up according to the second or third demon's fruit. So, you see, there is far more work involved than just to deal with the destroyers, although dealing with the

Strongman is the main work. It is the easiest of all. After we have the Strongman bound, Jesus says that we are then to **destroy** his goods -- 11Cor. 10:6.

Procedure for reproving
all works of darkness - Eph. 5:5-17

We are to reprove all works of darkness that they will be made manifest in the light, that they will clearly be seen and dealt with. Ministering spirits need to be called in to occupy the territory gained -- to keep out snipers, intruders, until a complete healing can be accomplished. Oil, laying on of hands, prayers of faith must be administered.

As children of light, (verse 8) we have a right to prove what we suspect to be hidden acts of evil, and look at them closely so that we may prove what is acceptable unto the Lord -- verse 10.

Seeing them in the Light of Truth we are better able to decide what the content is. Therefore, we must reprove them.

We might pray along these lines:

''I command that all of the dark works done in secret places of darkness and hidden from my eyes, and a shame to speak of, also all the evil spirits, human or demonic, involved in such works of darkness be made manifest (exposed, shown clearly, visible) in light to me, that I may view these works.''

Verse 13, whatever we see and decide is reprovable will be made manifest in light following our prayer of rebuke, censor, and blame, with which we charge and attack these unseen works and forces.

Once the dark works become manifest in the light, we must be prepared and willing to take the proper action.

Verse 11, Stop fellowship with unfruitful works of darkness that are being done in secret or mystery.

Last, but not least, after repentance, the Gospel Truth must be preached to them to seal the deliverance and completely free the victim.

So, you see, we have much to do in the spirit as first work which can be done silently from any distance. Also, much to do in the physical, but remember we are not the only ones working on this case. God has a **mighty** army awaiting to do battle.

"Are not all the ministering spirits to be sent forth for us -- the heirs of salvation?" Heb. 1:14.

SEND THEM FORTH!

12
A Bit of Wisdom to help the Seduced and Deceived

When I wrote the Book, "How to Try a Spirit", I did not teach on Seducing, Deceiving Spirits because God had not yet revealed the information that I have now. You can't teach until you've been taught!

Now I feel that I have some knowledge to share that would be of value to the ministry.

In addition to knowing the spirits by their fruit, I know their works. I have the solution that can lead to victory. "Ye shall know the truth, and the truth shall set you free!" Praise God.

I had been ministering to a couple who were involved in an occult group. The man was not as submitted to the group, as the woman. Through a Christian worker, he had found God, but his wife was in a state of apparent hopelessness. He took her to many churches and ministers but it seemed there was no one who could help her. He prayed, and fasted, and asked the Holy Spirit to lead him.

One night, sitting in a large auditorium listening to an evangelist, he noticed that two ladies in front of him were passing around and discussing a book. That book was my book on "How to Try a Spirit." He knew by the quickening of the Holy Spirit that it would contain the help he so desperately needed. He boldy told the ladies he must have that book. One of them sold him her copy.

After reading the book, with the hope that I would help his wife, he set out on the quest of locating me. He finally found me.

I knew that a person involved in false religions must be willing to submit to a long term ministry of healing, deliverance, and teaching. This is absolutely necessary for complete freedom. Knowledge of the Word of Truth is a primary safeguard against further deception.

Many are willing to submit to physicians and psychiatrists over long periods, but are not willing to stand still for sound doctrine. Read 1 Tim. 4:1

It is difficult to unlearn what is learned. False teaching must be dislodged. It must gradually be replaced with the doctrine of Christ...thereby involving the will of the person to submit to Bible study.

I told this couple that they did not get into this condition in a couple of sessions; but through many months of submission. Nor could they be helped in a couple of sessions; but they must submit to God faithfully until they could receive the truth of the Word and walk in it. They agreed, and were very faithful in attending all meetings.

After much prayer and teaching, the woman was still obviously possessed. She continously complained of a "numb feeling" in her head. It seemed that no matter how much we ministered to her, something was blocking our success. We desperately needed some special knowledge; a revelation from God.

One day, I was in a city where this particular occult group headquarters are located. I stopped for a light, and across the intersection in front of me walked dozens of young students leaving the building where they were studying these occult practices. I realized young people were being seduced into error by the score. As I looked at these clean-cut young faces, I cried out to the Lord, "God, help us to help them!" For some reason, we were ineffective against this particular demon's power.

Praise God, He heard me from His Holy hill! That very instant it was as though a curtain raised that I saw the wiles of the devil. I **saw** those lying devils working their strategy. I knew their inner-most secrets -- I knew the truth about them! Glory! And this truth was going to release the poor lady, and who knows how many others? Perhaps multitudes of deceived victims will be delivered and healed.

I drove back to the motel, and propped myself up in bed with pencil and paper. My God showed me the methods of the enemy all day long. He knows their every move. My God gazes upon their activities and brings them into confusion.

The Bible says that after the Holy Ghost has come, He will take the secret things of the Father and show them unto us. Glory to God in the highest who sees that His servants come behind in no good gift! Victory! In Isaiah 45: 3, 4 Amp., the Lord said:

> **"And I will give you the treasure of darkness and hidden riches of secret places, that you may know that it is I, the Lord of Israel, Who calls you by My Name!"**

The story as I see it

Every human being, especially the young, is on a quest. They know there are things unseen...yes, much more than meets the human eye. The Bible states that things which are seen are temporal, and things unseen are eternal. Think on this. They are seeking the Holy Ghost, but may receive an unholy spirit. (See first paragraph, pg. 4, **"THE HOLY GHOST AND MRS. GARRISON."**)

The angels have led the seeker to various ministries. They have sat in pews, and were bored with the programs. Since finding no spiritual help, nor reality there, they now seek elsewhere.

Satan can take care of this situation. He is not idle. He dispatches a "Seducing Spirit" to the seeker. The Seducing Spirit goes out with a certain task to perform. His strategic plan is to bring the seeker into a certain state of seduction.

That is the Seducing Spirit's mission, and he **always** does the same thing, even though in many different methods according to the case. (See Chapter 11).

One could clearly see why the man's wife had not been completely restored. After we bind the strongman, and loose his victim, the person is still left with this terrible wounded conscience that has been "burned" and then subjected to the infection of lies and false doctrine. As the conscience is that part that sorts out right from wrong, you can see why the victim has such a seemingly impossible chance of recovery without outside help.

I believe that the numb feeling was due to the Seducing Spirit's work to sear and wound her conscience. Casting out the demon is the easiest part of deliverance. Dealing with the damage he has done is the difficult part. In this case she had to have a healing. Her conscience would have to be restored to health, so that it could actively rebuke and resist the dark forces used by the cultist against those who dare to escape. (See Kingdom of Satan, Chap. 15.) Until this vital healing took place she could not hold her deliverance; without resistance they would take her at will.

I do not know how long it takes the Seducing Spirit to accomplish this terrible wound. But I know if one will give heed to him, he does succeed. It is only after the seeker finally chooses to submit to him and obey him that he can put the branding iron to the conscience.

Now when this job has been accomplished, he will call in the Deceiving Spirit, for he will not intrude into another spirit's ministry. (See "**THE FORMULA**" in "**THE HOLY GHOST AND MRS. GARRISON.**")

The Deceiving Spirit will have his own particular assignment to accomplish in the seeker, and a fertile field for it. Jesus has told us in the infallible test, that we may know the spirits by their fruits.

13

How the Seducing Spirit and the Perverse Spirit ministers to a homosexual

I am not qualified to know or understand what dark circumstances happened in a person's life to cause him to become a homosexual. I do not know what terrible wound was dealt to that human spirit to cause a gaping open hole in it that would not heal. It festered to the extent that this lonely soul would withdraw for awhile from what he would consider to be the ways of life. But I do know that this has happened to him, because the Lord of all the Universe has showed it to me.

I am highly qualified to write about what I do know to be true. I do so in the hope of ministering healing truth to those who are injured in their spirit, and have turned for hurtful reasons to a homosexual way of life. The truth is very important to those who are to receive this ministry because it is the key that will unlock the door that will let them go free. Please remember, as I present this truth, all good salve tends to sting a little as it is applied to open wounds. So stand still for the entire application, no matter how much it smarts. **For it is coming straight from the heart of a loving Father with a healing hand extended to the homosexuals.**

First, I am going to tell you some things about homosexuals that you will probably be very surprised to know. He will witness that they are true, but he may not be aware of the details. Here are some true facts:

1. He was created an equal human being in the likeness of God. Yes, the Father of all spirits put within him a **clear understanding** of the invisible things which **HE** made. He was born with a built-in knowledge of God's

eternal power and Godhead. He probably has never realized how valuable he is to the Creator. Perhaps, many times he cried out from the dregs of despair, ''Why?'' And he needs this true answer: Before the foundations of the earth were laid, Father God longed for children. He created all in His image for the express purpose of fellowship with them. Because of this purpose He put within him an intellect with spiritual powers and capacities of choice after His Own likeness, so that he could be a fit companion. He created man for His Own pleasure...Revelation 4:11.

2. But there is another in the picture -- Satan. He knows man's value to God. He desires to turn him against God. So he has laid certain snares that he has fallen into. He may think he has become a homosexual on his own, with no outside help, but another fact I am about to present to you will reveal the extent of outside influence involved in the homosexuals' present predicament. He is truly in a cell without bars. He is in a cell -- but there is a key. And it will let him out! But only the truth, if he receives it, will free him. Remember **truth** is the only key.

3. Here is how it happened: Two highly trained emissaries were sent from Satan with a specific mission. A Seducing Spirit was to do his job first, and if he succeeded, he would call in one stronger than himself, a Perverse Spirit, who would take over and bring him to his final state of imprisonment. The Seducing Spirit has a certain strategic plan. He knows that the victim has within him this ability to know the right way God has ordered things. This knowledge is seated in a part of the body we call the conscience. So naturally the main attack by the Seducing Spirit will be waged directly against the

conscience. The very first blow by that spirit was to "burn" the conscience, to "sear" it with a hot iron; to cauterize it, to render it unable to function.

It was only after the victim submitted his free will to participation in unseemly acts which are not convenient, but unnatural, that the Seducing Spirit was able to succeed in inflicting this terrible wound upon the victim, because at the first few submissions, the conscience convicted him, and God manifests His glorious creation--male and female, both having their natural function. And, because the victim did not like to retain God in his built-in-knowledge -- choosing to serve the creature more than the Blessed Creator, God, for this cause, gave him up as He would not intrude upon the free agency of choosing whom he would serve. When he "gave heed" to obey the Seducing Demon, only then could the demon put the branding iron to the conscience. After the mission of the Seducing Spirit has been successfully completed, **the Perverse spirit has moved in**, and is ready to begin his evil task.

A. Now, he also has a plan and will waste no time in putting it into action. His first work is to make a hole in the human spirit. How did he do it? Was it an abusing father he used? Was it terrible rejection by other males? He alone knows. But I am telling you the human spirit **was dealt** a mortal blow. No matter how it was accomplished, it was done.

B. Now -- as even a wounded animal will be dangerous and unpredictable, this terrible wound becomes corrupted, and causes this wounded human spirit to:

1. Rebel **against** God.
2. Fret against and hate God.
3. Dishonor their own bodies between themselves to strike out at God.
4. Become disobedient to parents.
5. Pervert the Gospel or Truth, twisting it

to Satan's advantage.

6. Make an all out surrender to wickedness, eventually causing one to be despised by themselves and others.

Finally, the Perverse Spirit will bring the victim to this point: ''Even though they know the judgment of God, that they who commit such things are worthy of death, not only do the same, but have pleasure in them, that do them.'' --- to the subverting of others. Because homosexuals have rebelled against God's righteous order to pervert it, it is necessary to learn that order, and be willing to totally accept it as right, ever seeking to know and walk upright before God.

So, now I bring to you **the good news...**

There has been a way of escape made for the victim. Help lies in a true conversion and decision to make a **total** commitment to Christ -- binding the Seducing and Perverse Spirits and casting them out. Call upon the Name of Jesus. ''For God so loved the world, that He gave His only Begotten Son, that whosoever believeth in Him should **NOT** perish, but have everlasting life. For God sent not His Son into the world to condemn the world; but that the world through Him might be saved.''

''Behold the **LAMB OF GOD**, which taketh away the sin of the world.''

When we acknowledge ourselves to be sinners, and take Jesus Christ as our Saviour, God gives us a new nature. We are born from above. ''Verily, verily, I say unto thee, Except a man be born again, he cannot see the Kingdom of God.'' By our acceptance of Jesus Christ as Saviour and Lord, we receive eternal life, for, ''As many as received Him, to them gave He power to become the Sons of God, even to them that believe on His Name. He that believeth on the Son hath everlasting life; and he that believeth not the Son shall not see life; but the wrath of God abideth on him. Verily, verily, I say unto you, he that heareth My

Word, and believeth on Him that sent Me, hath everlasting life, and shall not come into condemnation; but...**IS PASSED FROM DEATH UNTO LIFE.''**

Now, that **YOU** have heard this Word...would **YOU** say to **JESUS**, ''you have suffered in vain for me...**NO, THANK YOU? CHOOSE YE THIS DAY. CHOOSE LIFE.**

''Know ye not that the unrighteous shall not inherit the Kingdom of God? Be not deceived; neither fornicators, nor idolaters, nor adulterers, **nor effeminate, nor abusers of themselves with mankind**, nor theives, nor covetous, nor drunkards, nor revilers, nor extortioners, **shall inherit the Kingdom of God. And such were some of you; but, ye are washed, but ye are sanctified, but ye are justified in the Name of the Lord Jesus, and by the Spirit of our God.''**

SUCH MERCY!

14
Familiar Spirits

"Thou shalt not learn to do after the abominations of those nations. There shall not be found among you ANYONE... that useth divination, or an observer of times, or an enchanter, or a witch, or a charmer, or a consulter with FAMILIAR SPIRITS, or a wizard, or a necromancer. For ALL that do these things are an abomination unto the Lord!..." Deut. 18:9-12.

Those who divine by a Familiar Spirit are called:

Enchanter -- magician
Witch or Wizard -- one who practices witchcraft and sorcery, using Familiar Spirits to do their bidding.
Medium -- consulter with FAMILIAR SPIRITS
Clairvoyant -- witch or wizard
Necromancer -- one who consults the dead, wicked, unjust spirits.
Conjurer -- one who commands or summons Familiar Spirits to appear.

"Then said Saul unto his servants, Seek me a woman that hath a FAMILIAR SPIRIT, that I may go to her, and enquire of her. And his servants said to him, Behold, there is a woman that hath a FAMILIAR SPIRIT at Endor. And Saul disguised himself, and put on other raiment, and he went, and two men with him, and they came to the woman by night: and he said, I pray thee, divine unto me by the FAMILIAR SPIRIT, and bring me him up, whom I shall name unto thee."
Samuel 28: 7, 8.

Now a conjurer cannot summon the **just** spirits to appear since Jesus descended into hell where they were captive and released them from prison and carried them to Heaven, (Matt. 27: 52-53; Heb. 12:22). A conjurer may bring an evil **Familiar Spirit** from the same family to impersonate the just one. Being assigned to the family, this spirit will know all the personality traits of the "deceased just spirit." He will furnish the medium with the secrets that only the family members know.

The witch at Endor could bring up Samuel because he was held captive awaiting the Blood atonement or Cross work to be finished. Notice the Bible did not say the witch brought up an imposter, but Samuel himself. Just as a warden may take his keys and bring any prisoner you desire to see from his cell, providing he has him in custody. So can a medium who is "in authority" of Satanic power, have an evil spirit brought forth. She or he has power to use all the Host of Hell to do wicked supernatural acts in order to deceive and win over to Satan.

The Familiar Spirits cause paranoid, split personality. Because they are an innumerable class of evil spirits, each having a personality of his own, they seek to gain possession of living bodies and souls that they may express their own habits, personality traits, appetites, lustful desires, etc., thus we have what is called **SPLIT PERSONALITIES, THE PARANOID,** the possessed. When the living human spirit is completely overthrown, subdued, conquered, suppressed, and locked up in a cell inside the body and taken over, possessed completely by Familiar Spirits...then, we have the "insane."

The Insane

Insanity would be an end result of the individual work of the: 1. Spirit of Fear. 2. The Dumb and Deaf Spirit. 3. The Familiar Spirits. (See book, **HOW TO TRY A SPIRIT.**]

These first two spirits have completed their task in a victim and turned him over to the   Familiar Spirit to

65

possess. At this point the demons have attacked, struggled, wrestled, and gained control over the human spirit, the true possessor of the body, over a period of time. They have succeeded in entering, and capturing the spirit, binding it in order to control the mind and body. At times they will struggle with each other for momentary control of the body to express horrible acts of violence whether upon that body or others.

Manifestations (fruit) of the Familiar Spirits

Familiar Spirits are in charge of passing down every evil trait, genetic disease, evil inheritance of every unrepented sin visited down unto the third and fourth generation.

THEIR ASSIGNMENT is to visit:

1. curses.
2. the sins of the fathers.
3. unholy personal traits of the family.
4. inherited sicknesses and diseases.
5. evil habits.
6. tendencies.

THEIR ASSIGNMENT in the spirit world is:

1. to work in family blood lines.
2. to turn the family members from the paths of righteousness into everlasting punishment.

Unger's Bible Dictionary definition of Familiar Spirit: ''is a demon present in the physical body of the conjurer (a man or a woman.)

The term ''Familiar'' is used to describe the demon because it was regarded by the english translations as, ''A SERVANT BELONGING to a family, who was on intimate terms with the family possessing it,'' this indicates a parallel truth of the revelation to John that the departed brethren were ministering back and forth to their families, Rev. 19:10. Satan imitates this truth, assigning familiar

spirits to overthrow and bring family members into Satan's kingdom. The word "Familiar" means well-known.

It is a known fact that before a member of a family who has the Familiar Spirit dies, he or she decides just which family member is to receive the Familiar Spirit. This is called receiving the veil or mantle, (which is a counterfeit of the anointing.)

I have ministered to women who had this familiar spirit who were called to the death bed of their mothers and told to receive it, and felt it come into them as the mother died. A few were told that they were born with "the veil" over them and would be able to do divine acts by the Familiar Spirit.

A **FAMILIAR SPIRIT** is an evil family spirit who has managed to possess, gain entrance, or permission to dwell in a physical body. The Familiar Spirit will stay with the blood line until the line should die out, or they should be dismissed, cast out, and resisted. Only then will they seek another family.

If they are detected, renounced, and cast out of the family members they will enter into livestock belonging to the family in order to stay with the family. In case they may slip back in, or influence the family while off guard, (because of their assignment to that family).

These forboding spirits come and go at will if not resisted. They travel but may be readily summoned by the medium.

They are on intimate terms with the person possessed, anxious to serve and benefit them with supernatural tidbits in order to appease.

They have different degrees of intelligence, personalities, attributes, and talents. They will struggle over the opportunity to use the body they dwell in, that they might express themselves and their various talents.

What do the scriptures reveal about Familiar Spirits

Lev. 19:31   **"Regard not them that have Familiar Spirits."**
To honor, pay respect; support or associate
with them.

Lev. 20:6   The soul that does turn to them for advice and
knowledge shall be cut off with the Lord's face
set against them and their entire family,
bringing

Deut. 5:9   a curse to be visited unto the third and fourth
generation of their descendants.

Lev. 20:27   A man or a woman may have a Familiar Spirit.
God ordered those among His people stoned to
death, so that the others would not be defiled.

Deut. 18:10   The Lord told them after they came into the
land which the Lord gave them they should not
learn witchcraft. If one was among them, they
were to drive them out from them.

1 Sam. 28:3   Saul had put away those that had Familiar
Spirits. Saul went to the woman -- who had a
Familiar Spirit to bring back a spirit who was
familiar to him -- Samuel.

We are forbidden to have any traffic, fellowship, or
contact with these evil spirits, familiar or others. We are
forbidden by both the Old and New Testaments to give
them any place or contact other than "try the spirit" and if
it's not of God, resist it and cast it out of our families,
victims, etc., wherever we meet them. (1 John 4:1). These
are truly the dead spirits as they are under a curse, that we
are not to traffic with. Mediums do the exact opposite in the
seance.

Thoughts on Schizophrenia

As long as the human spirit is partially in control of his
own body and soul the spirits are sharing the facilities with
him. Unless resisted properly the spirits can take him at
will. Thus we have the Schizophrenic.

Mental disease -- characterized by disassociation from environment and deterioration of personality, split personalities -- more than one personality in one body. The human spirit is bound at times while the Familiar Spirits emerge, using the body.

Science has not yet found satisfactory answers for the two big questions about Schizophrenia: what causes it, and how it can be cured. While Science has not yet made that discovery, the Bible has it written down from the beginning. Yes, Christians who read and understand God's Word with His Spirit of Wisdom can tell you exactly what causes Schizophrenia and that the condition cannot be cured, except the Familiar spirits be bound and cast out first.

Therefore, Schizophrenia is one of those problems that should be treated by the clergy, as well as Medical Science. Though the Psychiatrist, by study of the psychic supernatural forces, may discover that the cause of the condition is demonic, unless he is filled with the Spirit of God, it would be dangerous for him to attempt to cast the spirits out. (Acts 19:14.) He is not dealing (or wrestling) with flesh and blood, but principalities of the air -- Eph. 6. Only those invested with the Spirit of God and the authority of His Name can successfully deal with demonic influences. Tranquilizing the poor human spirit only serves to render it even more helpless and weak, less able to do what it must do to resist the enemy.

The Spirit-filled knowledgeable worker can bind the strongman who produces that evil fruit, put them to flight by proper resisting forces. We are not to set about to cast out every demon we notice, nor to go into the asylums working in the flesh. The sons of God do the will of the Father. Those who cast out demons without direction of the Spirit are those who do not gather with the Lord, but scatter. These are those who will say to Him, ''Lord, you know me, I cast out devils in Your Name.'' and He will say, ''depart from Me, I never knew you.''

Our work demands that if we are led by the Spirit of God in our spirits, we are able with the finger of God to throw the evil spirits out of the soul, unbind the human spirit of man, and set it free from the captivity of Satan, giving that person an opportunity to repent and choose Life and Blessings instead of Death and Curses. After repentance and obedience it is of the utmost importance, that that person receive the Spirit of God into his spirit, because then he may be strong in the power of God which will enable him to further resist the evil spirits when they attempt to re-enter. Further, we are to teach Truth to the soul. Once Truth is known, it will set free. Knowing and quoting it to your soul and the evil spirits upon attack, will keep one free.

15
"The Way"
into the Kingdom of God,
the Holy of Holies,
the city of the Living God!

These next two chapters are a comparison of the two kingdoms, Kingdom of God, and Kingdom of Satan, to show how Satan tries to imitate God in every way.

At first glance the following material appears to be out of place, and not pertaining to our subject about evil spirits. But not so... one can hardly understand evil spirits without an overall knowledge of the real order of the spirit world and how each member functions in that world. It is **God's ordained order** about which we must learn the truth. With the veil rent in two, let the wise take a look inside.

This is the way, place, and position you must take in order to resist the Devil, as in James 4:7.

1. Submit yourself to God.
2. Resist the Devil.
3. He will flee from you.

The message of Hebrews is a revelation of God's complete and final work in Christ -- that is -- by faith we can accept the reality of an entrance into New Jerusalem itself -- through Christ.

The main thesis of Hebrews is Heb. 4: 14-16 -- that is, access to God and His throne room.

The new and living "way" is invisible, spiritual, the land of the real, fulfilling man's deepest needs! Heb. 12:22.

"The Way"

Isaiah prophesied "the way" both for spiritual and at the end of the age, literal.

Isaiah 35: 8-10; 60:11
> "And a highway shall be there, and a way, and it shall be called "The Way" of holiness; the unclean shall not pass over it; but it shall be for those: the wayfaring men, though fools, shall not err therein. No lion shall be there, nor any ravenous beast shall go up thereon, it shall not be found there; but the redeemed shall walk there: And the ransomed of the Lord shall return, and come to "Zion" with songs and everlasting joy upon their heads; they shall obtain joy and gladness, and sorrow and sighing shall flee away. Therefore thy gates shall be open continually; they shall not be shut day nor night.

ZION in the above verses and Hebrews 12:22, is the same one. We may go up in spirit until the city of the Living God comes down to us in reality at the close of the age.

Isaiah 57: 13b-15
> "But he that putteth his trust in Me shall possess the land, and shall inherit my holy mountain; And shall say, Cast ye up, prepare "The Way", take up the stumblingblock out of "The Way" of my people. For thus saith the high and lofty One that inhabiteth eternity, whose name is Holy; I DWELL IN THE HIGH AND HOLY PLACE, AND WITH HIM ALSO THAT IS OF A CONTRITE AND HUMBLE SPIRIT, to revive the spirit of the humble, and to revive the heart of the contrite ones."

Hebrews 9:8
> "The Holy Ghost thus signifying that the "Way" into the holiest of all was not yet made manifest, while as the first tabernacle was yet standing."

72

This is an old truth, but it is the new and living "Way" that Paul preached was the way into the presence of God.

Acts 24:14
"Paul said, "**But this I confess unto thee, that after the "way" which they call heresy, so worship I the God of my fathers, believing all things which are written.**"

Paul worshipped God by submitting to Him through the new and living "Way", the access into Zion, Heb. 12:22 -- opened up for us by Jesus.

"And so, dear brothers, now we may walk right into the very Holy of Holies where God is, because of the Blood of Jesus. This is the fresh, new, life-giving **"WAY"** which Christ opened up for us by tearing the curtain -- His human body -- to let us into the Holy presence of God. And since this great High Priest of ours rules over God's household, let us go right in, to God Himself, with true hearts fully trusting Him to receive us, because we have been sprinkled with Christ's Blood to make us clean, and because our bodies have been washed with pure water." Heb. 10: 18-22 LB

In the Old Testament days, a veil was hung before the sanctuary where God was, and only the chosen Priest could enter into God's presence. A rope was placed around his ankle in case he fell dead, he could be removed.

"The old agreement didn't even work. If it had, there would have been no need for another to replace it. But God Himself found fault with the old one, for He said, "The day will come when I will make a new agreement with the people of Israel and the people of Judah. This new agreement will not be like the old one I gave to their fathers on the day when I took them by the hand to lead them out of the land of Egypt; they did not keep their part in that agreement, so I had to cancel it. But this is the new agreement I will make with the people of Israel, says the Lord: "Heb. 8: 7-10 LB. When Jesus Christ gave up the

Ghost, the veil of the temple was torn in half -- from the top to the bottom. When the veil was rent in two, He opened up the **WAY** into the Holy of Holies. Now Blood-washed people can come right on in to their God. Yes, the likes of you and I, through the Blood of Jesus can walk right up boldly to the throne of God Almighty!

So... in studying the book of Hebrews, we find it is an established fact that since Jesus opened up this "**WAY**", we **can** go in now.

What should we expect to find when we take this privileged "trip"? To answer that question, let us turn to Hebrews 12:22...

"**But you have come right up into Mount Zion, unto the city of the living God, the heavenly Jerusalem,**"...

Wow... you mean we can go into new Jerusalem **NOW**?... that's what the Book said. Also, that we could sit down together with Christ Jesus when we get there **WELL!**... Eph.2:6.

Who else will be there?

"**and to the gathering of countless happy angels;**" LB

Imagine so many angels you cannot count them. **Who else will be there?** Heb. 12:23 KJV!

"**and to the general assembly and church of the firstborn, which are written in heaven.**"

Who are the firstborn? All of the Old Testament saints to the thief on the cross. All of those converted before the Blood was shed. These saints make up part of the multitude of captives Christ captured from Satan when He descended into the underworld, where all the just departed spirits were held prior to the atonement. Jesus took these captives with Him when He ascended on high. Eph. 4: 8-10; Heb. 2: 14-15; then, according to Matthew 27: 51-53

"And, behold, the veil of the temple was rent in twain from the top to the bottom; and the earth did quake, and the rocks rent; And the graves were opened, and many bodies of the saints which slept arose, And came out of the graves after His resurrection, and went into the holy city, and appeared unto many."

Now, when Christians die they no longer go into the lower parts of the earth, but to the New Jerusalem!

'Who else is there?

"and to God who is Judge of all;"

Here is the One to whom Job cried, "Oh, that I knew where I might find Him! That I might come even to His seat! I would set my cause in order before Him, and fill my mouth with arguments." Job 23:3 A.S.V.

What Job longed after is **our** glorious priviledge. We may come boldly, with confidence that we will not be consumed by such majestic splendor that we might make our petition known to our great and glorious Father. Oh, what grace!

Here is the center of all reality!

He really did create us for His fellowship then: Yes... hold on to your wig now... Heb. 12:23.

"and to the spirits of just men made perfect."

You mean... my righteous Mom... Uncle Tom and Aunt Jane? Certainly! As many as died justified by the blood of Christ will be there. But... I thought we were not allowed to contact the dead? We aren't. **These are not dead, but alive forevermore** having obtained eternal life. Matthew 22: 29-32, in part, says, "God is not the God of the dead, but the God of the living. Ye, therefore do greatly err." Isn't that a fact? Most of our false thinking and action comes

75

from not knowing how it is. When Jesus said, **"Let the dead bury their dead!"** -- Matthew 8:22 -- He knew the just had no dead! They had only taken up residence in the New Jerusalem! The Book said we could assemble together into fellowship with **all** the departed righteous. This **is** the assembly of God!!

Who Else?

"Jesus the mediator. One who brings about a reconciliation between all these participants of the New Covenant." Jesus is your representative that negotiates all your throne rights and benefits of the Scriptural promises that are being appropriated by you. (Jesus Blood spoke better than blood of animals that Abel had to offer, "A new and better way, walk ye in it.) "And to the Blood of sprinkling, that speaketh better things than that of Abel." **OK**... now, **what are all these "spirits of just men made perfect"** doing?

Surely they don't just sit around heaven all day. No. Besides this great Host of Heaven assembly, each party has their own particular assignment to perform in bringing about the will of God on earth as it is in Heaven. There is much written on the ministry of Angels, and all these other parties mentioned in this assembly. But not much on the duties of the departed brethren. **Are there any Bible accounts given?**

Yes... let us take a look at a few.

Rev. 5:5 -- One of the elders, a redeemed man, spoke to John. Rev. 7: 13-15 -- A departed brother asked a question of John while John was on the earth, and gave him the answer. Rev. 19:10 -- This being, told John he was a fellowservant which proves he was a redeemed man, free to come and go from heaven to earth, ministering to the needs of saints. And probably even more surprising to you at this point, he further revealed to John this: "And of **thy brethren** that have the testimony of Jesus." (Only humans can have the testimony of Jesus.) Thy brethren usually meant a relative in their household or family as: The House of Jacob, David, Hur, etc... which could infer that these spirits are ministering within their own families. See Rev. 22: 8-9.

Let's return to Hebrews 12:25, which says:

"See that ye refuse not **him that speaketh. For if they escaped not who refused him that spake on earth, much more shall not we escape, if we turn away from him that speaketh from heaven."** KJV

This is a **warning** to those who refuse and oppose the truth of this Blood Covenant to enter into this rest and those who would forsake the fellowship of the New Jerusalem.

Hebrews 4: 1-3a, 6, 11, 15, 16 -- **"let us therefore fear, lest, a PROMISE BEING LEFT US OF ENTERING UNTO HIS REST, any of you COME SHORT OF IT. For unto us was the Gospel preached, as well as unto them: but the Word preached did not profit them, not being mixed with faith in them that heard it. For WE WHICH HAVE BELIEVED DO ENTER INTO REST. Seeing therefore it remaineth that some must enter therein, and they to whom it was first preached entered not in because of UNBELIEF:"**

Sometimes patient endurance is necessary to obtain the promises of God. Heb. 6:15.

Jer. 6:16, who spoke and said:

"Thus saith the Lord, Stand ye in "The Way", and see, and ask for the old paths,where is the good "WAY", AND walk therein, and ye shall find rest for your souls. BUT... THEY SAID "WE WILL NOT WALK THEREIN!"

The book of Hebrews is God's complete, full, and effective revelation of the work of His Son Jesus Christ. The recipients of it must beware of the refusal to enter in.

Let us labour therefore to enter into that rest, lest any man fall after the same example of unbelief. For we have not an High Priest which cannot be touched with the feeling of our infirmities; but was in all points tempted like as we are, yet without sin. Let us therefore come boldly unto the **throne of grace**, that we may obtain mercy, and find grace to help in time of need.

This is the secret place of the Lord, and those that find it are renewed in knowledge after the image of Him that created him. Col. 3:10.

For here is hidden all the treasures of wisdom and knowledge of God. Col. 2: 3, 9.

And we all may come into His very presence through the **BLOOD!** Now... Come and go with me to my Father's house!!

''**And the ransomed of the Lord shall return, and come to ZION with songs and everlasting joy upon their heads: they shall obtain joy and gladness, and sorrow and sighing shall flee away.''** (Isaiah 35:10)

SO... COME WITH ME TO MT. ZION, THE CITY OF THE GREAT KING!

With what attitude should we enter into His presence?

With Holy boldness. Making a joyful noise, come before His presence with singing! Enter into His gates with thanksgiving, and into His courts with praise! Be thankful unto Him, and bless His Name -- Psalms 100.

Exalt the Lord thy God, and worship at His Holy hill -- Psalms 99:9.

When Isaiah had his tremendous vision in the Temple, he must have forseen our glorious privilege of entrance into His presence through the Blood of Jesus. He said, ''I saw also the Lord,... high and lifted up, and His train,

78

(Wedding Garment) filled the Temple." The Seraphim is there crying, "Holy, Holy, Holy, is the Lord of Hosts: the whole earth is full of His glory." He went into that vision by faith, just as we, by faith, must come into His rest -- Hebrews 4: 9, says: **"Let us, labour therefore to enter into that rest, lest any man fall short by unbelief."** Unbelief will block our "Way" into the presence of God.

When you do come into his presence, realize:

There is no distance between you and God; that you are with God; that you are not speaking to the top of the ceiling, or sky, which cannot hear, but to God whose ear is open to your plea.

So... speak boldly with all honesty, for you must worship Him in Spirit and Truth. Your spirit goes in; your flesh stays on earth. The things you see will be with spiritual eyes. The more faith and trust you have in God's Word, the more awareness you will have of Him. Your experience of being near Him will be more vivid. If you are not fully convicted of the validity of this truth, you may not discover this reality because of unbelief and doubt.

Before Jesus made the Blood sacrifice and sent the Holy Ghost to dwell with us forever, man did not have this fresh, new, living way into His presence.

How do you do it?

Before you go, take a little time of preparation. After all, you take time to dress, wash your face, brush your hair before you go to church. Even so... examine yourself:

1. Does anyone have ought against you? Go and reconcile to him, if possible.
2. Any unconfessed sin in your life? Confess it, and repent, that it may be washed in the Blood that was shed for the giving up of sin.
3. Forgive everyone his trespasses against you, that God will forgive yours.

Now... submit yourself to God! You cannot effectively resist the Devil if you do not know the correct way to submit yourself to God.

A Guide Line Prayer

Now To — **Jesus Christ**, who by the renting of the veil, the tearing of Your Own body, this entrance is made possible. I praise You, Jesus, for opening up the new life-giving way. I confess my sins and faults before you now, and ask You to blot them out with Your Blood; that I shall be white as snow, justified in the sight of my Father. I could not come to my Father God, except by You, Jesus. I give You honor and glory for this unspeakable gift. It is only right that Your Name be lifted above every name! Oh..., Jesus, my Great High Priest, who rules over God's household, I adore You, I thank You, My Lord!''

. . . .

Speak a word to the countless happy Angels.
''I thank all of you for your ministry to me. Thanks for encamping round about to guard me, for leading sinners to me for Gospel work that I am to do, and for your aid to me in battling the hosts of hell!''

. . . .

Greet the General Assembly and Church of the Firstborn.
''Ask Daniel just how he felt about those lions. Or perhaps talk to Joshua about the grapes. Ask Lot about Sodom and Gomorrah...whatever!''

. . . .

Say hello to all the redeemed: ''the just men made perfect!'' To all your family and friends. Yes, say hello to all who are assembled in the gathering; to all whose names are written in the Lamb's Book of Life.

Hallelujah!

. . . .

And now to God, the Judge of all spirits in Heaven and Earth: ''You are the Greatest of All, the Almighty, the All knowing, Ever present, Immutable God! The Creator of the world, the sun, the light, the night, and of man himself. Let everything that has breath,

Praise ye the Lord!

Now...

Let your request be made known unto God! And you know **IF** He hears you -- and **HE** does! You **have** your request.

What happens when we go into the Holy of Holies, when we go into New Jerusalem, the city of the Living God?

In my Father's presence is fulness of joy: At His right hand there are pleasures forevermore -- Psalms 16:11.

For since the beginning of the world men have not heard, nor perceived by the ear, neither hath the eye seen, Oh God, beside thee, what He hath prepared for him that waiteth for Him. -- Isaiah 64:4. This is the unlimited realm of His presence!

David **foresaw** ''The Way'' into the presence of God. It is a marvelous thing to hide under the shadow of His wings and to be the apple of His eye -- Psalm 17:8.

Psalms 36: 7, 8: "How excellent is thy loving kindness, O God! therefore, the children of men put their trust under the shadow of thy wings. They shall be abundantly satisfied with the fatness of THY HOUSE; and thou shalt make them drink of the river of thy pleasures. For with thee is the fountain of life: in thy light shall we see Light."

In the presence of God, some of the things that happen:
- Times of refreshing.
- Restitution of all things which have become twisted, perverted, spotted from the world, damaged, and worn.
- We are made to know wisdom in the hidden man.
- There God writes His laws in our heart,
- and makes us want to obey Him.
- There we hear joy and gladness, for no sorrow may enter His gates.
- There our human spirit is renewed within us, for it has become blemished with unbelief and doubt.
- There we are cleansed.
- A right spirit is renewed within us.
- There we are restored to the joy of His salvation.
- There we receive His free spirit (The glorious liberty of the sons of God who are led by His Spirit, and do His will.)
- There we receive instruction, messages, teachings, revelation, information, and answers, unlimited knowledge.
- There we find mercy for ourselves and grace to help others - Heb. 4:16.
- In Thy presence is renewed strength - Isaiah 40: 28-31
- For it is **only after** we have dwelt in Thy presence, that we can teach transgressors Thy "Ways:" and sinners can be converted unto Thee - Psalms 51:13.
- Yes, it is only **after** you have come near the Lord that you should speak, teach, and convert - Isaiah 41:1.

If we continually use our rights to go through the Blood into the presence of God Himself, we will come to have a close relationship with God. He knows us and we know Him. There are people who say they know God who do not know Him personally as they could, nor are interested enough to read all about Him. Those are the ones who will say, "Lord, Lord, you know me, I have cast out devils in Your Name." And He answers, "Depart from Me, you workers of iniquity. I know you not. If you are not working **with** Me, You are scattering!"

If He gives you the invitation and right to visit Him as often as you like, and you never get around to it, you neither love Him nor know Him.

A Haven for the Weary Soul

Tired of the heat of the Battle?
Afflicted on every side?
There is a rest for the weary,
A place... where the soul can hide.

The unredeemed are talking about soul travel
Projecting their soul into the Cosmo.
But I know of a place in the heavens,
Where only the righteous can go!

Most are waiting til hereafter
They could walk right in if they knew.
Some may never discover,
But the details are found in Hebrews.

The cross of Calvary finished it.
Let me tell you where it's at,
You take some steps to repentance
and a bath in a blood-filled vat!

Now... walk right in dear brothers
without nary a nod
For THAT bath made you eligible...
For the Holy presence of GOD!

NOW THAT'S SOUL TRAVEL

by Mary Garrison

16
"The Crooked Way" into the Kingdom of Satan, parallel truth, imitated, counterfeited "Way" for his followers

"The Crooked Way"

Isaiah 59: 1-8

"The way of peace they know not; and there is no judgment in their goings; they have made them CROOKED paths; whosoever goeth therein shall not know peace. Behold, the Lord's hand is not shortened, that it cannot save; neither his ear heavy, that it cannot hear: But your iniquities have separated between you and your God, and your sins have hid his face from you, that He will not hear. For your hands are defiled with blood, and your fingers with iniquity; your lips have spoken lies, your tongue hath muttered perverseness. None calleth for justice nor any pleadeth for truth: they trust in vanity, and speak lies; they conceive mischief, and bring forth iniquity. They hatch cockatrice eggs, and weave the spider's web: he that eateth of their eggs dieth, and that which is crushed breaketh out into a viper. Their webs shall not become garments, neither shall they cover themselves with their works: their works are works of iniquity, and the act of violence is in their hands. Their feet run to evil, and they make haste to shed innocent blood: their thoughts are thoughts of iniquity; wasting and destruction are in their paths. "THE WAY" of peace they know not; and there is no judgment in their goings: they have made them CROOKED paths; whosoever goeth therein shall not know peace.''

Key to understanding the kingdom of darkness

The greatest and most important work of Satan now among men is to counterfeit the **KINGDOM OF GOD**, deity, reign, city, "**The Way**", the doctrine, worship, experiences, gifts, miracles, religion, fasting, all Bible principles, procedures, etc...

To simulate all the attributes, ways, and things of God so as to **deceive** mankind.

Just as the Bible sets forth a pattern of proper approach to God, so the Devil desires that those who seek his allegiance come to him in the same manner he has designated. All occult ritual is based on this premise. Satan desires not only to be like God, but to be God. Therefore, he seeks to imitate God in every way, also producing an imitation of every attribute and gift. He simulates the things of God by counterfeit. (Isaiah 14:14.) Because of this fact, we can know what his strategy and setup is like.

I will endeavor to show the **comparison**, parody, parallel reversal, opposite; the twisting, perverting, counterfeiting, simulating ways and methods of the adversary -- Satan. The reversal of the normal, right, and accepted methods.

God has His own city -- the New Jerusalem, located in the heavens, (See Chapter 15, The City Of God, And How to Get There). It is set up in righteous order. Satan has his city -- the Principality of the Air, (Eph. 6:12). It is set up in unrighteous order.

God has His order, the Godhead, chief princes, archangels, etc., who rule different kingdoms and planets -- on to the living human beings: ministers, consecrated servants, etc., who **do** the will of God.

In comparison, Satan has his order, evil angels and rulers of the darkness of this world on to the wicked living: the mediums, witches, unjust, etc., who **do** the will of Satan. Human spirits who are alive are of the utmost importance to both kingdoms. They are the just and the unjust.

Comparison of soul travel for the just and unjust

As we see in the chapter entitled "The Way" to the City of God," the living **just** are given a glorious entrance into the very presence of God, that we may go in and out, (Heb. 22:23) through the Blood of Jesus.

The **unjust** living are given a like opportunity of ascending in spirit to the very presence of Satan, himself, projecting his spirit into his presence, also by a blood sacrifice. This ritual may be performed by offering human or animal blood.

God required the blood of a spotless lamb. Satan requires the blood of a very evil sacrifice, such as filthy menstrual blood, the goat or pig, or perhaps human blood. Evil abominable things are used to obtain Satan's presence and favors -- the opposite of the Lamb of god. Remember, the **key** to observe is that they do the opposite, the reversal of the right. Heb. 10:19.

According to Heb. 10:22, the righteous are required to draw near to God with:

1. A true heart -- honest, earnest, sincere.
2. Full assurance of faith -- positive convictions and belief.
3. Hearts sprinkled from an evil conscience, (the inner man or spirit sprinkled by the Blood of Jesus.)

On the other hand, the wicked draw near to Satan with the opposite:

1. A false heart -- unfit, insincere.
2. Wavering doubt and unbelief in truth.
3. Heart full of evil, seared conscience -- (the flesh sprinkled by the blood from the evil sacrifice.)

They work their evil with such abominable things as: Lapping blood, froth from the mouth of a person or dog possessed with a dumb and deaf demon (mad), guts, snakes, spit, and exact opposite to God's requirements for His blessings.

In Heb. 12: 22-24
 The righteous come unto Mt. Zion,
  city of the living God, the heavenly Jerusalem,
   to an innumerable company of angels,
    to God the Judge of all,
     to spirits of just men made perfect,
      to Jesus the mediator of the new covenant,
       Blood sprinkling that speaketh better things
        than that of Abel.

The unjust wicked living have access into the kingdom of Satan by means of soul travel.
     project their spirits into the principalities and powers
     of the air which is Satan's domain and city,
       to a company of evil angels, evil princes,
        common demons, strongman spirits, etc.
         familiar spirits, the cursed and the damned
          down through the ages, whose names are written
           in Satan's book of death,
            and finally to Satan, the adversary of God,
             and man.

Yes...

The wicked, through the blood of sacrifice, trans-cendental meditation, soul travel, astro-projection, etc., may come unto the seat of Satan in the air... the **unholy of unholies.**

More parody observation

The sons of God do the will of the Father -- God.

The sons of Satan do the will of their father -- Satan.

Knowing that Satan desires for himself that which pleases God, witches take Scriptures, and Scriptural principles from the Bible for their purpose to twist, pervert, and reverse them to Satan's advantage. Seeking to please and appease Satan, they render such things that God requires of the just, to Satan.

Some examples of this:

The Lord's prayer may be twisted thus by the children of Satan: "Our Father, which art in the earth..."

Words and Prayers:

The Word of God spoken by a righteous person mixed with faith, and the will to do the will of God -- avails much good.

The Word of God perverted by an unrighteous person, mixed with evil intentions, and the will to have their own way, will do the will of Satan -- and avail much evil.

Words are very important to witches in pronouncing curses, hexes, spells, etc. The "words" which make a spell, hex, or curse work for the magician are handed down from magician to magician, or witch to witch. They believe that the **spoken word** mixed properly with **the will, belief,** will bring about what is stated, a perverted principle of "believe and you shall receive," believing in the accomplished work of Christ and a will to do the will of God.

Another Bible principle counterfeited by the witch is:

The prayer of faith used by the righteous -- speaking forth the Word of God, believing it, and a will to do His will, "If ye abide in Me, and My Words abide in you, ye shall ask what ye **WILL**, and it shall be done unto you." Witches, using this principle unto Satan, also believe and **WILL**.

"Now faith is the substance of things hoped for, the evidence of things not seen," another example of the so - called faith imagination:

Concentrated imagination -- mental pictures of what the witch wishes to come to pass. Thoughts are projected toward the victim, actually conjuring up a mental vision of the evil that he desires for the victim.

Will power -- takes unto captivity a negative, submissive, weak, unstable, unfaithful, off-guard, dull person; constantly and unrelentlessly strives to bring one into servitude to the witches' own will.

Another attempt to imitate by Satan is:

God sends the Comforter and Helper, the Holy Ghost to dwell within a born-again child to lead and guide him into all Truths. By the Holy Spirit we are endued with power from on high to do divine acts.

Satan imitates this action by assigning an unholy spirit, called a spirit guide, to live in his followers to lead and guide him into all untruth -- this Spirit of Divination endues the person with power from "on high" to do divine acts by the Familiar Spirits.

Remember, the **KEY** to understanding all the kingdom of darkness, and how it works is a **reversal** of Christian methods. Satan simulates the methods of God.

What is Witchcraft?

Witchcraft is a work of the flesh of the witch using evil spirits to produce the evidence. This work may consist of whatever strategy, artifice, method, subtlety, beguiling trick, ingenious clever device the witch may choose, contrive, or design to bring about the witches' (man or woman) evil purposes, or **will.**

The witch chooses the procedures to be used to charm, ensnare, mislead, divert, and overthrow the victim.

The choice could consist of any number of ways or means, such as: potions, rigmaroles, magic charms, incantatious, ceremonies, psychic projections, etc.

What power does the witch employ?

The psychic or witch has power. We need to correctly assess and recognize the extent of that power, because many battles have been lost because of an underestimation of the strength of the enemy. Do not continue to ignore them, hoping they will go away. They intend to wax worse and worse as the age draws to a close. Only proper Scriptural resistance will make them flee.

The psychic or witches' power consists of all the powers and energies of man, all the Satanic power they can call, or summon up (the familiar spirits), to please their perspective master -- Satan.

All witches are power hungry. There are no neutral forces. Behind every inflow of power dwells a supernatural being. The spirits can work apart from the medium, but not as effectively as they can with a body to use. So can God work apart, but He has chosen to work through man when He can.

When a witch, medium, or psychic does a work of the flesh, such as: Pronounce a curse, a spell, a hex, a charm, or their psychic projections on an object, that work they do will remain standing until a stronger power supercedes it. Read Luke 11: 21, 22. Can you see the importance of Christians being knowledgeable of these things, and using the power that has been given us over all the power of the enemy? It is not enough to read Luke 10: 19, we must **use** it!

Make no mistake about the witch. They are children of the Devil -- submitted, committed, sold out, enemies of **all righteousness**! They stalk their prey with exceeding cunning. It is folly to refuse to fight them with **ALL OF OUR STRENGTH**! They are working their **evil will** upon **us** -- the end of which is to see our souls destroyed!

What are some of the symtoms of Psychic Attack?

Extreme weariness, confusion of the mind -- mental fatigue, anxiety, distress -- disconnected thoughts -- dull, trancelike or spaced out emptiness -- loss of self-control over mind as the witch seeks to take captive the mind, bringing it into subjection to the witch -- as in hypnotism. The victim may suffer accidents, loss of income, position, and reputation, or may be afflicted with diseases and pain, according to the witch's desire.

Among the witches' abilities may be the powers to reach any given object at whatever distance, with an irresistible will over the elements. It appears the measure of the individual witch's strength depends upon how many demon spirits they can summon who will obey their commands.

Evil familiar spirits are called from the principalities of the air to go and bind the victim. They are given specific commands and instructed as to the **exact will** of the witch, who is a medium of Satan.

May a Christian unknowingly use Psychic Power?

Yes, that's why we need to study to show ourselves to be a worker approved of God, and we will not need to be ashamed, rightly dividing the Word of Truth. Many Christians actually do not know the difference between psychic prayer and power, and Godly prayer and power!! In obedience to Acts 19:19, ''let all the Christians who use ''curious arts'' bring all their books together and burn them before other Christians, no matter how costly they may be!'' The above verse shows that Christians were guilty then, and still are. Psychic prayer is a heathen counter-part of Christian prayer. Those who fool around with craft (not Gospel procedures), cannot inherit eternal life. Ga. 5: 20-21.

What must we do?

The unrighteous are doing these tremendous and mighty exploits. Christians should be doing exceeding miracles over all that the evil ones can do. For they can only counterfeit the great works of our God, and they learned that by studying and trying to apply the **reversal** of the Word of God! Perhaps that is our explanation of why the church is not prevailing, some do not get around to even reading the Word of God, much less applying it to their lives. Jesus, Philip, Peter, Paul and many others down through the march of history have done miraculous feats.

The evil ones are busy using psychic power against the President of the United States, the FBI and all those who are in authority. I just read an account where an organized group of witches calling themselves a church, has declared war on the FBI and the United States Government! They actually penetrated secret government files. People, our government has no chance of fighting this kind of power with flesh and blood! They have no idea of what they are up against. That is why we, the Church, are to pray for those in authority first in our meetings. 1 Tim. 2: 1-3.

We can work the works of Jesus!

LET'S GIVE THEM THE WORKS!

Remember that **EVERY POWER** must yield to the risen Christ! We are accused of being demon hunters and chasers, so let us live up to it! Let us take our mighty weapons and stalk the roaring, devouring lion and get him! Why be the hunted when we can be the hunters?!!

These powerful weapons were given to us for offense. Only the protective armour is for defense!! Let's **offend** the enemy! Not one another! It is for sure that if the enemy is hunting you, the reason is that he wants to devour you!

1. Resist the Devil and he will run from you. Don't stop there -- chase him -- then launch an all-out powerful attack against him! Don't be lazy, we must be valiant! Bind up Satan's strongmen, destroy his goods -- pull down his strongholds -- nullify his works, cleanse his victims, heal the sick, set them free. Work the works of Jesus that will remain forever. Isaiah 47: 12-14. Get into the heat of the battle or get spewed out of God's mouth for being lukewarm!

2. Stop fighting other brethren! A house divided against itself cannot stand!! Stop fighting the brethren who are fighting the Devil! Band together with them. Num. 32: 6b, 7, says:

"Shall your brethren go to war, and shall ye sit here? And wherefore discourage ye the heart of the children of Israel from going over into the land which the Lord hath given them?"

God has endued His people with far superior powers and abilities than the psychics can hope to attain. With that power we are to let the oppressed go free, break every yoke, undo every burden, and loose all the wicked bonds put on people by the witch, psychic or satanic forces. We must **take** our power over them, reversing the action by superior "Power over all their power", or they will remain in bondage. Luke 10:19. It is our job. God said, **you** do it, using the Name of My Son, Jesus. How many do you think God can find who will stand up and be counted in this warfare? Those who dare will be counted very valuable, important to God in this work!

Yes, the evil ones are performing their spectacular works which are seducing and enticing thousands to become interested. On the other hand, the Christian is given power over all their power, to do greater **works** than Jesus for this same purpose: (John 14:12) to interest, influence and meet the needs of mankind that is more than sufficient. Yet the seeker has already tried the church and came out feeling the Christian needed more help than he! A form of Godliness, denying the **power** of God!

Do not be guilty of refusing to acknowledge God's unlimited power that is necessary to bring in the Kingdom of God, but get into the New Testament and put the principles of Christ into action, start raking in the results.

A guideline of prayers offered when ministering to those under psychic attack

OPENING PRAYER: I come to you, Lord, as my deliverer. You know all my problems, all the things that bind, that torments, defiles, and harasses me. I refuse to accept anything from satan, and loose myself from every dark spirit, from every evil influence, from every satanic bondage, from every spirit in me that is not the Spirit of God, and I command all such spirits to leave me now. I confess that my body is a temple for the Holy Spirit, redeemed, cleansed, sanctified, justified, by the Blood of Jesus. Therefore, satan has no place in me and no power over me through the Blood of Jesus.

Loosing from domination

In the name of Jesus Christ, I now renounce, break, and loose myself and all our children, from all psychic heredity, demonic holds, psychic powers, bondages, bonds of physical or mental illness, or curses, upon me or my family line, as the result of sin, transgressions, iniquities, occult, or psychic involvements of myself, my parents, or any of my ancestors, of my spouse, any and all ex-spouses, or their parents, or any of their ancestors. **I THANK YOU LORD, FOR SETTING US FREE.**

Loosing from curses, spells

In the Name of Jesus Christ, I now rebuke, break and loose myself, and all our children, from any and all evil curses, charms, vexes, hexes, spells, jinxes, psychic powers, bewitchments, witchcraft, or sorcery, that have been put upon me, or my family line from any person or persons, or from any occult source. **THANK YOU, JESUS, FOR SETTING US FREE.**

Releasing a ministry from psychic commands

Devils, witches, and cohorts,... I see that you are harrassing and embarrassing this ministry; attempting to smear and discredit so as to discourage others who would receive benefits from this ministry. I am not ignorant of your tricks, wiles, and strategy. Now I command you to stop your operations, that all of your psychic commands, incantations, prayers, and desires against this ministry be turned again upon you who sent them out. That you retreat, flee in defeat this moment. I also command that the mouths of all who help spread lies against this ministry be stopped. **THE LORD REBUKE YOU AND ALL WHO HELP YOU. IN JESUS NAME.**

The Chart

Understanding the Kingdom of Darkness depends upon understanding the spirit world, God's creation, His righteous order, His plan for man and world, His final overthrow of Satan and his entire Kingdom of Darkness and all his followers. Knowing the Truth about all of this is what produces co-heirs with Chirst; it is this Truth that frees; it is this Truth that overcomes the enemy on **every** realm and level; it is the knowledge of this Truth that allows us to understand all the other Truths in full, and allows us to function in harmony with God and all His Heavenly Host, to confront and defeat Satan and the Host of Hell through the victorious Cross work -- the atonement, the access opened up through the shed Blood, the keys to the Kingdom -- which is -- binding and loosing!

Every realm, classification, operation, law, or system in the Kingdom of God has its' Satanic substitute in the Kingdom of Darkness.

The following chart is not meant to present a complete picture, but to show how Satan tries to imitate God in our comparison of the Two Kingdoms.

KINGDOM OF DARKNESS
Descending to Babylon (principality of the air)
Headquarters & seat of Satan.

THE HOST OF HELL

Satan, the father of all liars

Anti-Christ 666, incarnation of Satan

The living wicked unjust suedo under rulers, who are the

mature Child of the Devil, who do the will, of their father; who have the use and authority of his name, spirit, power, dominion, sacrificial blood, and likeness. Also to share in Satan's eternal damnation and death!

False apostles	False pastors	Sorcerers
False prophets	False teachers	Mediums
False evangelists	Adepts	Magicians

The Moral Sinner

The wicked unjust dead

The Familiar Spirits -- whose assigned job is to work in the family blood line; to visit evil traits, curses, inherited diseases, help overthrow and bring people unto Satan, etc.

The Evil Angels, Strongmen Demons, Princes over all planets, nations, cities, countries, and communities.

Common demons -- who carry out the orders of the above, etc.

Living Creatures -- who knows what Satan has made in his attempts to create -- clones? Frankensteins? Monsters?

The animal kingdom -- demon possessed animals.

THE TWO . . . .

THE PARALLEL TRUTH OF THE . . . .

KINGDOM OF GOD
New Jerusalem (Descending City)
Capital of the Universe.

THE HOST OF HEAVEN

God, the Father of all spirits

Jesus Christ, the Lord

The living righteous just, under rulers -- the

Sons of God, who do the will of the Father, who have the use and authority of Jesus' Name, His Spirit, His power, His dominion, His Blood, His Flesh, His strength, His Word, His Likeness, His Eternal Life -- those who have JESUS:

Apostles	Teachers
Phophets	Lay Ministers
Evangelists	The Spirit-Filled
Pastors	

The Carnal Babes

The righteous just dead -- spirits of just men made perfect.
Heb. 12:22.

The Ministering Spirits --- whose job is to work in their family blood line; to visit blessings, earned rewards, inherited good traits of the righteous to thousands of descendants of those who loved God -- help to win and bring them to God, etc.

The Arch-Angels, Gabriel, Michael, etc. -- rulers over planets, nations, cities, countries, and communities.

Common angels -- who carry out the orders of the above parties.

Living Creatures -- Seraphim, Cherubim, Zoa, who knows?

The animal kingdom -- spirit animals and living creatures.

. . . . KINGDOMS

. . . . PHYSICAL AND SPIRIT WORLD . . . . AS I SEE IT!

Dear Reader:

After reading this book, if you agree with us that the Body of Christ needs this information, would you please help us to distribute **HOW TO TRY A SPIRIT,** the sequel, **HOW TO CONDUCT SPIRITUAL WARFARE,** and **THE HOLY GHOST AND MRS. GARRISON,** by:

1. Giving one to your friends.

2. Asking your local book store to order them.

3. Sending them to Missionaries, and people elsewhere who need the information to minister to others.

4. Send contributions to aid us in advertising and postage.

5. Make suggestions as to how we can better advertise and distribute.

6. Send us addresses of those who may like a brochure.

CHRIST CAMP MINISTERIES is a non-profit organization. Your contributions are tax deductable.

Thank you for any help you feel led to give.

His servant,

Mary Garrison

Mary Garrison

$3.95

The Holy Ghost and Mrs. Garrison

by Mary Garrison

THE HOLY GHOST AND MRS. GARRISON is an easy-to-read narration spotlighting the HOLY SPIRIT of God as HE works to lead and guide us into great truths.

"...I had this quest in my soul to fully know this invisible Person who actually lived within me..."

After reading THE HOLY GHOST AND MRS. GARRISON, one will agree that she was successful in capturing HIS humorous personality at work and sharing it with us.

You will laugh and cry as you also get to know HIM and HIS ways through Mrs. Garrison's experiences. Best of all, you will discover that you have unconsciously been lifted into a greater faith yourself!

by MARY GARRISON

How To Try A
SPIRIT
by their fruits you
will know them.

by Mary Garrison

HOW TO TRY A SPIRIT is really an unveiling of evil spirits and their work. It is intended to be an aid in recognizing the principal evil spirits that are now working the world. These evil ones so closely *IMITATE* the Spirit of God, that we must learn to *try them by their fruit*, else the elect of God may be deceived.

This book was written as an easy reference, so that one may quickly find the Bible name of a particular evil spirit; a list of his fruit underneath the name; a short discussion of some of the methods employed by that spirit, and finally the Scriptural method we are to use in dealing with him.

This work has helped many to quickly make positive indentification of the various evil spirits, thereby avoiding deception by them. *HOW TO TRY A SPIRIT* will enable one to effectively aid others who have unknowingly allowed these evil spirits to stay and produce fruit in their lives.

Many ministers and Gospel workers have testified that they have found this work an indispensable aid that always proves to be a *WORKABLE TRUTH* in trying a spirit.

by MARY GARRISON

BINDING, LOOSING, AND KNOWLEDGE are the KEYS TO THE KINGDOM OF GOD!

As a Christian we must know more about these KEYS and how to use them. Why? Because Jesus gave them to the BELIEVER to bring in the KINGDOM OF GOD.

This book will help you to understand how to use them properly. It is the fourth volume in the deliverance series, revealing additional information on evil spirits not revealed in the other books. It gives the Bible name of the spirit, the fruit that they produce, and the profile of the person in which the spirit lives and operates so that he can be easily recognized.

Also in this book are important revelations to the Body of Christ that gives a step by step procedure in the ministry to the oppressed. This book will prove to be another indispensible guideline for the GOSPEL WORKER, an extension of applicable knowledge contained in the first three volumes.

PLEASE REMIT PAYMENT WITH ORDER IN U.S. DOLLARS

	copies	each	extension
PLEASE SHIP AT ONCE:			
"How To Try A Spirit"	_____	@ $ 6.95	_____
"How To Conduct Spiritual Warfare"	_____	@ $ 6.95	_____
"The Holy Ghost and Mrs. Garrison"	_____	@ $ 6.95	_____
"Keys to the Kingdom are Binding, Loosing, and Knowledge"	_____	@ $ 6.95	_____
All 4 Books for $25.00 Donation	_____	@ $25.00	_____
		Sub-Total	_____

PLEASE ADD CORRECT POSTAGE & HANDLING. _____
(SEE CHART)   TOTAL _____

NAME _____

STREET ADDRESS _____

CITY _____ STATE _____ ZIP _____

Postage & Handling	
Add 50¢ per item for Canada	
$ 9.99 or less	$2.50
$10.00–$19.99	$3.00
$20.00–$29.99	$3.50
$30.00–$39.99	$4.00
$40.00–$49.99	$5.00
$50.00 or more	$6.00

Southern Victory

Christ Camp Ministries, Inc.

P.O. Box 158
Chelsea, AL 35043